THE WORLD WAR II
QUIZ & FACT BOOK

THE
WORLD WAR II
QUIZ & FACT
BOOK

TIMOTHY B. BENFORD

HARPER & ROW, PUBLISHERS, New York

Cambridge, Philadelphia, San Francisco, London
Mexico City, São Paulo, Sydney

1817

For my wife, Marilyn

FIRST EDITION

Designer: Sidney Feinberg

Library of Congress Cataloging in Publication Data

Benford, Timothy B.
  The World War II quiz & fact book.
  Bibliography: p.
  Includes index.
  1. World War, 1939–1945—Miscellanea. I. Title.
II. Title: World War 2 quiz and fact book. III. Title:
World War Two quiz and fact book.
D743.9.B464   1982   940.53   82–47516
                                            AACR2
ISBN 0–06–015025–4   82 83 84 85 86 10 9 8 7 6 5 4 3 2 1
ISBN 0–06–090978–1 (pbk.)   82 83 84 85 86 10 9 8 7 6 5 4 3 2 1

Contents

Foreword

Well before it ended, the Second World War was recognized as the single event that affected more lives than any other in human history. More than four decades after it began, there is hardly a person alive whose life has not in some way been directed or altered by its consequences. Books and films covering every aspect of the conflict have continued to be enormously popular. Millions of words, in a multitude of languages, retrace the various campaigns, examine closely the political and military leaders, and attempt to enlighten an audience now accustomed to watching history being made while sitting comfortably in its living room.

But, even if the convenience of television had been available for remote coverage of the conflict, it is very likely that all those books and all those words would have still been written about it. Beyond its scope and size, World War II was different, perhaps a psychological turning point in the evolution of mankind, bringing about an awakening of human interests and feelings unlike any war preceding it. It is even possible that the classification of events as being pre- or post–World War II will eclipse the time standards of B.C. and A.D. in measuring mankind's often flawed progress on this planet. It may not happen in this century, or even this millennium, but it will happen. Provided we don't first destroy earth in a final holocaust.

Between 1939 and 1945, events took place that changed our lives. Sometimes they happened in the chambers of power in Washington, Berlin, London, Tokyo, or Rome. More often than not they happened on a beachhead, in a forest, on a previously unknown island, or in the ruins of a devastated city. Enormous numbers of people died, twice as many civilians as military personnel. Many of those who survived came out of the war with determination to change the course of future history, and have been trying with various degrees of success ever since.

This book ventures to present both the great events and the trivial, if anything about world war can be considered trivial, as a collection of facts, vignettes, and occurrences. Not only is it informative and entertaining, it also makes vividly real once again the details of a great convulsion that shook the world, with all the human tragedy—and the occasional saving humor—that accompanied it.

Introduction

There was never a problem of what to include. The problem was what not to put in. As one can imagine, there is an abundance of anecdotes, vignettes, items of interest, facts and just plain trivia that came out of the war years. However, space does not permit use of it all.

I began this project by collecting information of an unusual or extreme nature. There are over 1,000 pieces of information in question-and-answer form plus 50 photographs and the Appendix. Some of the material shatters popular myths, but the majority of it underscores the folly of war. Nothing here is original, save the information I gathered from individuals who participated in the war, and I suspect that even much of that has previously been recorded elsewhere. My co-authors of this work are the people listed in the bibliography. My task was to edit their labors for this presentation. And herein may exist my future frustrations: contradictions.

Despite the millions of words written about the war, despite the talents of some of the leading historians of this century, contradictions abound. I've spent an extraordinary amount of time checking and confirming various details that appear differently in major works. Sometimes this happened when information was published too soon after the war and in later years was corrected by other authors. Every effort has been made here to publish the most accurate and confirmed information available. If the reader finds an error, it is mine and mine alone.

U.S. Coast Guard Photo

FACT: Approximately 700 journalists followed U.S. forces in all theaters of the war. Over 450 participated in the Normandy invasion on D-Day alone. This photo, taken on Iwo Jima, shows a series of foxholes scooped in the volcanic ash that served as a press and photo headquarters for newsmen covering that conflict. Empty ration boxes served as desks for the Coast Guard combat photographers. Small sign says "Iwo Jima Press Club."

Multiple Choice

Q. Identify the type of aircraft that was produced in larger amounts than any other during the war.

    a. Japanese Zero
    b. Messerschmitt BF-109E
    c. B-24 Liberator
    d. DC-3 (including C-53 and C-47 versions)

A. The Messerschmitt BF-109E, with nearly 36,000 produced.

Q. Which American entertainer traveled the most to entertain troops during the war?

    a. Gary Cooper
    b. Bob Hope
    c. Joe E. Brown

A. Joe E. Brown traveled over 150,000 miles. He was named Father to All Men Overseas by the National Father's Day Committee in 1944.

Q. Which unit was nicknamed the Red Devils?

    a. Russian Sixth Army
    b. U.S. 1st Infantry
    c. British 6th Airborne

A. The British 6th Airborne.

Q. Identify the only U.S. Navy ship sunk by enemy gunfire on D-Day.

    a. U.S.S. *Corry*
    b. U.S.S. *Augusta*
    c. U.S.S. *Butler*

A. The *Corry,* by gunfire from German gun batteries on Utah Beach. Thirteen members of her 294-man crew died.

Q. Identify the first U.S. Army Air Force aircraft type to see action in Europe.

    a. Grumman Wildcat
    b. Lockheed P-38
    c. Douglas Havoc

A. The Douglas A-20G Havoc, a ground attack bomber, on July 4, 1942.

Q. How did U.S. Admiral Thomas C. Hart, commander-in-chief of the Asiatic fleet, depart from the Philippines on December 26, 1941?

    a. Russian fishing boat
    b. U.S. submarine *Shark*
    c. P-40 Flying Tiger, which he flew

A. Via the *Shark,* headed for Java, where the Asiatic fleet was reorganizing.

Q. Identify Hitler's chauffeur.

    a. Victor Lutze
    b. Erich Kempka
    c. Hugo Blaschke

A. Kempka. Lutze was Hitler's SA chief of staff and Blaschke was the Fuehrer's dentist.

FACT The flag that flew aboard the U.S.S. *Missouri* during the surrender ceremonies in Tokyo Bay on September 2, 1945, was the same flag that had flown over the U.S. Capitol in Washington, D.C., on December 7, 1941.

Q. Identify the first U.S. Navy ship named in honor of a black.

> a. *Emmons*
> b. *Harmon*
> c. *Baldwin*

A. A mess attendant killed saving his shipmate's life during the Guadalcanal campaign, Leonard Roy Harmon was posthumously awarded the Navy Cross and was the first black to have a ship named in his honor. His mother christened the destroyer escort *Harmon* on July 25, 1943.

Q. Who commanded the Big Red One during the Sicily campaign?

> a. George Patton
> b. Walter Bedell Smith
> c. Terry Allen

A. Terry Allen commanded the U.S. 1st Infantry Division, the Big Red One.

Q. What was the U.S. VI Corps code name for the plan to break out from Anzio by way of Cisterna and Valmonte, Italy?

> a. Buffalo
> b. Crawdad
> c. Grasshopper

A. Buffalo. Crawdad was the plan to go along the coast to the northwest. Grasshopper was the plan for an eastward breakout. The plan to go via Campoleone was Turtle.

FACT The 130-ton white plaster cast model of the U.S. Marine Corps War Memorial remained in sculptor Felix de Weldon's Warwick, Rhode Island, studio from 1954 until October 1981. The bronz sculpture was unveiled at Arlington National Cemetery in 1954, but no home for the plaster original was found until de Weldon donated it to the Marine Military Academy. Valued at $3.5 million, the 108-piece model takes four months to assemble. It was delivered to the MMA in Harlingen, Texas, by nine eighteen-wheel flatbed trucks. Dedication was on February 19, 1982, the thirty-seventh anniversary of the assault on Iwo Jima.

Q. Which Russian newspaper did Soviet troops prefer for rolling cigarettes?

    a. *Pravda*
    b. *Izvestia*
    c. *Red Star*

A. Red Star had a reputation for burning better and as a result was more popular.

Q. Who said, "He who holds Paris holds France"?

    a. Charles de Gaulle
    b. The Duke of Windsor
    c. Adolf Hitler

A. Hitler.

Q. Who was the last commander of the Afrika Korps?

    a. Jurgen von Arnim
    b. Sepp Dietrich
    c. Gustav Fehn

A. Von Arnim was commander of Axis troops in North Africa, Dietrich was an SS panzer commander in the Normandy and Ardennes campaigns. The last commander of the Afrika Korps was General Gustav Fehn.

Q. What was the unofficial name for the allied ships' assembly area as they got under way for the French coast in June 1944?

    a. Piccadilly Circus
    b. Swine Lake
    c. Hero Harbor

A. Piccadilly Circus.

FACT   For a time during the Battle of Britain RAF pilots were ordered to destroy German air-sea rescue seaplanes marked with the Red Cross, to prevent the rescued German pilots from fighting another day. The order met stiff resistance among RAF pilots.

Q. Which tank was produced in greater numbers than any other?

    a. German Panther
    b. British Churchill
    c. American Sherman

A. There were only 384 Panthers built and 5,640 Churchills. Of the twenty-six different tank models used by both Allies and Axis powers, the Sherman, with 49,000 units made, was by far the leader. Russia produced 40,000 T34/76 tanks for number two position. Despite its high production numbers, the Sherman got low grades as a weapon. Some 3rd Armored Division commanders called them "deathtraps."

Q. Where did the largest tank battle in history take place?

    a. Tunisia
    b. Ardennes Forest
    c. Kursk

A. Around the Kursk salient in July 1943, where the Russians and Germans employed approximately 3,000 tanks. Germany lost more than 400 tanks in the conflict.

Q. What was the name of the bridge at Sant'Angelo, Italy, over the Rapido?

    a. Brooklyn Bridge
    b. London Bridge
    c. Mussolini Bridge

A. London Bridge.

Q. Which was the only major surrender after D-Day that was *not* accepted in the name of the Allied powers?

    a. Rome
    b. Paris
    c. Berlin

A. Paris. It was accepted in the name of the Provisional Government of the French Republic, according to instructions de Gaulle had given General Leclerc.

Q. The first Allied troops to cross the Strait of Messina and set foot on the Italian peninsula were under the command of:

    a. Mark Clark
    b. Bernard Law Montgomery
    c. George Patton

A. The Eighth Army, under Montgomery, did it on September 3, 1943.

Q. How many .50-caliber machine guns were on board B-17 Flying Fortresses?

    a. Eight
    b. Thirteen
    c. Between fifteen and twenty

A. Thirteen.

Q. How many Japanese troops were killed trying to prevent the U.S. from retaking the Philippines in 1945?

    a. 100,000
    b. 250,000
    c. 450,000

A. The Japanese lost 450,000 troops.

Q. When did the U.S. *officially* declare that war with Germany had ended?

    a. May 7, 1945
    b. January 1, 1946
    c. October 19, 1951

A. October 19, 1951. Britain, France, Australia and New Zealand declared war with Germany as officially ended on July 9, 1951.

FACT The first British air raid of the war, on September 6, 1939, resulted from a disastrous false alarm. British Spitfires mistakenly shot down two British Hurricanes. There were no German aircraft over England.

Q. When did Japan sign the peace treaty with the U.S. and forty-eight other nations (except the U.S.S.R.), officially ending its role as a belligerent?

    a. August 15, 1945
    b. September 2, 1945
    c. September 8, 1951

A. September 8, 1951, at San Francisco, California.

Q. How many of the 2,000-plus German Navy crew members survived the sinking of the battleship *Bismarck?*

    a. Less than 50
    b. 110
    c. Almost half

A. The British rescued 110 German sailors and officers.

Q. How many aircraft did Japan produce during the war?

    a. 35,000
    b. 65,000
    c. over 80,000

A. Approximately 65,000, of which 9,000 were left at the end of the war.

Q. When did Josef Stalin become Premier of the Soviet Union?

    a. 1927
    b. 1931
    c. 1941

A. On May 7, 1941. Though he controlled the U.S.S.R. well before that, he had not held the title of Premier.

FACT British commandos who crossed the English Channel and attacked Germans in France (killing two) the day the German-French armistice was signed were almost prevented from landing back in England because they carried no identification. One boatload was delayed at Folkestone harbor for several hours.

U.S. Army Photo

Q. Identify the island on which war correspondent Ernie Pyle was killed.

    a. Okinawa
    b. Iwo Jima
    c. Ie-shima

A. Seen here with a tank crew of the 191st Tank Battalion, Fifth Army, in the Anzio beachhead area in Italy in 1944, Pyle was killed on the Pacific island of Ie-shima, off Okinawa. Pyle is seated center, with goggles, in photo.

Q. How many Russian aircraft were destroyed by the Germans during the first seventy-two hours of Operation Barbarossa?

    a. None
    b. Under 1,000
    c. Nearly 2,000

A. The Germans succeeded in destroying approximately 2,000 Russian planes in what had only three days earlier been touted as the largest air force in the world.

Q. Which Nazi is credited with issuing the first order for the extermination of Jews?

    a. Himmler
    b. Goering
    c. Ribbentrop

A. Goering, in a letter to Reinhard Heydrich on July 31, 1941, in which he asked for a "final solution of the Jewish question." (This is the earliest known *written* order.)

Q. What were British casualties in the sinking of the aircraft carrier *Ark Royal?*

    a. One
    b. Half the crew
    c. All

A. One casualty. She sank on November 14, 1941, two days after being torpedoed by U-81 off Gibraltar.

FACT   After the war it was learned that the U.S. shot down Japanese Admiral Yamamoto's plane with the help of Ultra intelligence. The British charged that the U.S. compromised the security of the code-breaking, but the U.S. denied the charges and defended its position. Previously secret wartime messages released to the U.S. National Archives in 1981 substantiate the British position. American fighter pilots talked over the air so much about the Yamamoto incident that the Japanese suspected their codes were being read and immediately changed them. It took four months for the U.S. to crack the new code.

Q. How many aircraft carriers did Japan lose during the war?

    a. Ten
    b. Twenty
    c. Thirty

A. Twenty, including five escort carriers, between May 7, 1942 (*Shoho* in the Battle of the Coral Sea), and July 24, 1945 (*Kaiyo* in Beppu Bay, Japan).

Q. Which Italian city was subjected to the worst bombing raid (in Italy) of the war?

    a. Rome
    b. Naples
    c. Turin

A. Turin, on November 20, 1942, by the RAF.

Q. When did the U.S. Eighth Air Force bomb Berlin for the first time?

    a. 1942
    b. 1943
    c. 1944

A. On March 4, 1944, three months before the Allied invasion of France.

Q. Who was Supreme Allied Commander, Mediterranean Theater?

    a. General Sir Harold Alexander
    b. General Carl A. Spaatz
    c. General Sir Henry Maitland Wilson

A. Wilson. Alexander was commander of Allied armies in Italy, and Spaatz was commander of U.S. Strategic Air Forces in Europe.

FACT   The U.S. 2nd Armored Division employed a tank equipped with a loudspeaker rather than guns to get German villages and towns to surrender. Lieutenant Arthur T. Hadley, a psychological warfare specialist, commanded the tank.

U.S. Army Photo

Q. Name the first American general to command four field armies.

     a. Dwight Eisenhower
     b. Louis A. Craig
     c. Omar N. Bradley

A. During the drive into Germany the First, Third, Ninth, and Fifteenth armies were under the command of Omar N. Bradley. Their combined strength was nearly a million men. In this November 1944 photo, Eisenhower, Craig and Bradley (from left to right) appear delighted with the war's progress as they meet in Butgenbach, Belgium.

Q. Name the German general who while chief of the Luftwaffe general staff committed suicide because of abuse and scorn he received from Hitler.

    a. Hans Jeschonnek
    b. Robert Ritter von Greim
    c. Ernst von Falkenhausen

A. Greim committed suicide on May 24, 1945. He had replaced Goering as head of the Luftwaffe; but it was Jeschonnek who as chief of staff was unable to tolerate the abuse from Hitler and ended his own life on August 18, 1943. Falkenhausen, who served as governor-general in occupied Belgium and northern France, was a conspirator in the July 20, 1944, plot to kill Hitler.

Q. Which Axis power suffered most from the Allied use of incendiary bombs?

    a. Germany
    b. Japan
    c. Italy

A. Japan by far. Building construction in Japan was over 80 percent wood and wood product, while in Germany stone and brick were the primary building materials. However, the U.S. and Great Britain dropped almost a million and a half incendiaries on Hamburg, Germany, in July and August 1943, causing the infamous "firestorms."

Q. What was responsible for the loss of the one and only U.S. lighter-than-air craft during the war?

    a. A German U-boat
    b. Bad weather
    c. Friendly fire

A. U-boat 134 gained the distinction of shooting down the only airship lost by the U.S. during the war when it successfully defended itself from attack by Airship K-74 off the Florida Keys on July 18, 1943.

Q. Which Allied general was code-named Duckpin?

a. Devers
b. Eisenhower
c. Truscott

A. Supreme Commander, Allied Expeditionary Force in Europe, General Dwight D. Eisenhower was Duckpin.

Q. Identify the first type of naval vessel captured by a U.S. Navy boarding detail in the war.

a. Japanese destroyer
b. Italian destroyer
c. German U-boat

A. On June 4, 1944, U.S. Navy Captain Daniel V. Galley of the U.S.S. *Guadalcanal* sent a detail to board German U-boat 505 off the African coast. It was the first enemy ship so captured since 1814. Abandoned by its crew, U-505 was towed to the U.S.

Q. Who said, "At the moment the situation in Italy is such that not a single Luftwaffe aircraft dares show itself"?

a. U.S. General Carl Spaatz
b. Luftwaffe chief Hermann Goering
c. British Air Chief Marshal Sir Arthur Tedder

A. World War I air ace and Luftwaffe commander-in-chief, Reichsmarschall Hermann Goering on May 28, 1944. He made the pronouncement to Hitler.

Q. The U.S. 93rd Infantry Division was:

a. All American Indian
b. All black Americans
c. German-speaking Americans

A. It was an all-black American division.

FACT   U.S. submarines sank more enemy tonnage than all other naval and air combatants combined.

Q. Where did the Germans launch their last panzer offensive in North Africa?

 a. Djebel Bou-Aoukaz
 b. Maknassy
 c. Medenine

A. The successful assault by German armored units resulted in the capture of Djebel Bou-Aoukaz, Tunisia, on April 30, 1943. The attack had begun on the 28th.

Q. When was General Eisenhower named Supreme Commander, Allied Expeditionary Force?

 a. 1942
 b. 1943
 c. 1944

A. On Christmas Eve, December 24, 1943.

Q. Which country suffered the greatest merchant marine losses in the war?

 a. Britain
 b. Japan
 c. Germany
 d. U.S.

A. Britain, with 4,786, was followed by the others: Japan 2,346; Germany 1,595; U.S. 578. A total of 11,700 merchant ships of all nations were sunk between 1939 and 1945.

Q. How long after Britain declared war on Germany was it before RAF planes flew over Germany?

 a. The same day
 b. Not for three months
 c. Almost one year later

A. The same day, September 3, 1939. The RAF dropped six million propaganda leaflets on northern German cities but no bombs.

Q. When did the first Allied air raid on Germany take place?

    a. The day after war was declared
    b. One month after the start of war
    c. Not until the end of "the phony war"

A. The day after war was declared, when RAF bombers flew toward Germany's North Sea navy bases. However, of the twenty-nine planes in the mission, seven were shot down, ten couldn't locate their targets, one bombed neutral Denmark by mistake and three bombed British ships in the North Sea. Eight planes succeeded in reaching their targets but did little damage.

Q. The Anglo-American organization responsible for gathering intelligence in the Middle East was known as:

    a. The Ankara Committee
    b. The Cairo Committee
    c. The Suez Section

A. The Ankara Committee. The other two are fictitious.

Q. The name of the Allied operation to capture Sardinia was known as:

    a. Brakestone
    b. Brimstone
    c. Stonewall

A. Brimstone.

Q. When did Italy formally declare war on Germany?

    a. It didn't
    b. In September 1943, when the Allies invaded
    c. In October 1943

A. King Victor Emmanuel read the declaration on October 13, 1943, and Italy was then recognized "officially" as a co-belligerent by the Allies.

FACT Once Italy joined the Allies against the Germans, only seven of its sixty-one divisions were actually involved in combat.

Q. The first Italians to fight as Allied co-belligerents were in the:

    a. Army
    b. Navy
    c. Air force

A. The 1st Italian Motorized Group became part of the U.S. Fifth Army on October 31, 1943.

Q. What was the code name for the Canadian attack on the so-called Hitler Line in Italy?

    a. Camel
    b. Chesterfield
    c. Lucky Strike

A. Chesterfield.

Q. Who was the commander of the Hermann Goering Division in the Sicily campaign?

    a. Major General Paul Conrath
    b. Lieutenant General Adolph Steiner
    c. Brigadier General Carl Muller

A. Major General Paul Conrath. The other two are fictitious.

Q. Who was Carl Johann Wilberg?

    a. An Allied spy in Berlin
    b. Admiral Canaris's code name
    c. A BBC broadcaster who spoke German

A. An Allied spy who remained in Berlin up to the end informing on troop movements and conditions. He was a member of the Office of Strategic Services (OSS).

Q. Which Allied nation can claim that its ships were the vanguard of the Normandy invasion?

    a. France (free forces)
    b. United States
    c. Britain

A. Britain. Twelve minesweepers cleared the waters close to the French shore on June 5 at night.

Q. Who said, "Paris is worth 200,000 dead"?

  a. A German General
  b. A British politician
  c. A French Resistance leader

A. "Colonel Rol," of the French Resistance.

Q. General Chaing Kai-shek was code-named:

  a. Moss Bank
  b. Kingpin
  c. Peanut

A. The Allied code name for French General Henri Giraud was Kingpin. French Premier Pierre Laval was Moss Bank. Peanut was the official code name for Chiang Kai-shek. It was also the nickname U.S. General Joseph Stilwell used to display his contempt for the Chinese leader.

Q. What was the production rate that the American aircraft industry reached in 1944?

  a. One plane a day
  b. One plane every hour
  c. One plane every six minutes

A. One plane every six minutes!

Q. Which U.S. division is credited with securing the first U.S. beachhead in France?

  a. 1st Infantry
  b. 4th Infantry
  c. 29th Infantry

A. The 4th Infantry Division on D-Day.

FACT Hitler had two horoscopes,—one from November 9, 1918, and the second from the day he took power, January 30, 1933—that predicted the outbreak of war in 1939, victories until 1941, difficulty in April 1945 and peace in August. Both horoscopes also noted that Germany would begin to rise again in 1948.

Q. Identify the Frenchman who is credited with bringing information to the Allies that led them to change plans and liberate Paris.

    a. Roger Gallois
    b. Charles de Gaulle
    c. Georges Eugène Haussmann

A. Gallois succeeded where even de Gaulle failed. Haussmann, appointed by Napoleon III, had designed the "modern" Paris with its broad and beautiful boulevards.

Q. Who accepted the surrender of the German commander of Paris when the city was liberated?

    a. A French lieutenant
    b. An American GI
    c. A British medic

A. Lieutenant Henri Karcher "of the Army of General de Gaulle" accepted the surrender of General Dietrich von Choltitz.

Q. What was the name of the directional device used to correct RAF bomber accuracy by sending a beam from England?

    a. Elbow
    b. Oboe
    c. Hobo

A. Oboe.

Q. What was the nickname given to the machine the British built to decode messages they received on the Enigma code machine?

    a. The Bomb
    b. The Thing
    c. Our Friend

A. The Bomb.

FACT Hitler's bunker in Berlin was surrendered to the Russians by Luftwaffe doctor Captain Walter Hagedorn.

Q. How many Allied ships did German U-boats sink between 1939 and 1945?

    a. 1,400
    b. 2,800
    c. 3,900

A. More than 2,800, at a cost to Germany of 630 U-boats and 27,491 submariners.

Q. When did the Polish Navy surrender to the Germans?

    a. October 1, 1939, a month after war began
    b. The crews scuttled their ships instead
    c. It didn't have a chance to surrender

A. October 1, 1939. However, some ships made their way to Britain and sailed with the Royal Navy.

Q. Where did the idea for partitioning Germany after the war originate?

    a. Britain
    b. France
    c. U.S.A.
    d. Soviet Union

A. On January 15, 1944, a cabinet committee that was chaired by future Prime Minister Clement Attlee in Great Britain made the recommendation.

Q. On May 13, 1944, an American destroyer escort sank a Japanese submarine that was:

    a. Carrying a peace offer to the U.S.
    b. Returning to Tokyo with plans for an atom bomb that it received from Germany
    c. Operating in the Western Hemisphere

A. Japanese submarine Ro-501, one of the few of its class to operate in the Western Hemisphere, was sunk. There were no peace offers or atom bomb plans aboard.

U.S. Army Photo

Q. Name the U.S. general who said, "When the going is tough, in a brawl or battle, there is no better fighting partner than the man from Down Under."

        a. Matthew Bunker Ridgway
        b. Robert Lawrence Eichelberger
        c. Joseph Stilwell

A. General Robert L. Eichelberger, commenting on the spirit and ability of the Australian troops in the Buna campaign. He is seen here inspecting a Japanese saber at Mokmer Airstrip, Biak Island, Dutch New Guinea, on June 30, 1944.

Q. What was the Allied code name for the U.S. Army?

    a. Destiny
    b. Challenge
    c. Force

A. Destiny.

Q. Identify the European city that was proclaimed an open city on August 14, 1943.

    a. Prague
    b. Lourdes
    c. Rome

A. Rome. However, the Vatican was bombed by Allied aircraft on November 5.

Q. What was the Allied code name for the Russians?

    a. Laundress
    b. Ecuador
    c. Ali Baba

A. Laundress was the name of the Vichy French. The Greeks were known as Ecuador in Allied codes. Ali Baba was the code name of the Russians.

Q. How did Polish General Wladislaw Sikorski die?

    a. In an airplane crash near Gibraltar
    b. As a suicide in England
    c. Facing a Russian firing squad

A. Sikorski and several other Polish exile leaders were killed in a plane crash near Gibraltar on July 4, 1943.

FACT A Jewish battalion from Palestine fighting in North Africa was almost totally wiped out during the German offensive against Bir Hacheim in June 1942. Less than fifty of the just over 1,000 troops survived. The Palestinians, along with Free French troops, kept the Germans from reaching Tobruk.

Q. Which country sent in the first troops to assist the Partisans in Yugoslavia?

    a. U.S.
    b. Great Britain
    c. Soviet Union

A. The first assistance for Tito's communist Partisans came from Great Britain in May 1943.

Q. What German site was the target of the first major daylight air raid on the Ruhr?

    a. Gestapo headquarters
    b. A synthetic rubber plant
    c. Port facilities

A. The synthetic rubber plant at Huels.

Q. Where was the site of the only wartime meeting between Generals Douglas MacArthur and George Marshall?

    a. Washington
    b. Goodenough Island
    c. Tokyo

A. On Goodenough Island off New Guinea.

Q. Luftwaffe efforts to supply Axis troops in Africa resulted in fifty-one transports and sixteen escort fighters being shot down in a period of less than fifteen minutes, an event that was known as

    a. Bloody Sunday
    b. Palm Sunday Massacre
    c. The Europe-to-Heaven Run

A. More than seventy U.S. and RAF fighters, supplied with Ultra intelligence, easily mauled the Germans on Palm Sunday, April 18, 1943, in what became known as the Palm Sunday Massacre.

FACT Messerschmitt designed two long-range bombers *named* after the city that was their intended target: New York.

Q. When did the U.S. officially declare its neutrality after war began in Europe?

    a. It didn't
    b. September 5, 1939
    c. December 7, 1939

A. September 5, 1939.

Q. What was the code name for the German air and sea invasion of Crete?

    a. Mercury
    b. Silver
    c. Gold

A. Mercury.

Q. Prime Minister Winston Churchill's plan for an invasion of northern Norway was known as:

    a. Mars
    b. Jupiter
    c. Saturn

A. Jupiter.

Q. The B-29 that dropped the first atom bomb on Japan was part of:

    a. Special Services, Pacific
    b. 509th Composite Group
    c. Allied Pacific Air Wing (APAW)

A. The 509th Composite Group, Twentieth Air Force. (The plane was named *Enola Gay*. See Appendix for what became of her.)

Q. German casualties from the Allied raids on Dresden on February 13–14, 1945, were:

    a. 35,000
    b. 100,000
    c. 135,000

A. One hundred thirty-five thousand people were killed.

Q. Who captured the German High Command headquarters at Zossen?

    a. Patton's Third Army
    b. Montgomery's Desert Rats, the 7th Armored
    c. Rybalko's Soviet 3rd Guards

A. Colonel General Pavel Rybalko's 3rd Guards captured the headquarters intact. However, the German senior military personnel had moved to Rheinsberg, about fifty miles northeast of Berlin.

Q. Identify the last German strongpoint in Paris to surrender on liberation day, August 25, 1944.

    a. The Louvre
    b. Notre Dame
    c. Luxembourg Palace

A. Luxembourg Palace, home of the French Senate, at 7:35 P.M.

Q. How many aircraft did the Russians employ when they began their attack across the Oder that began the Battle of Berlin on April 16, 1945?

    a. Under 2,500
    b. About 6,500
    c. Over 9,000

A. About 6,500, which came in to finish the job started by the thirty-five-minute artillery bombardment.

Q. Who was head of the American OSS in France in August 1944?

    a. Colonel David Bruce
    b. Joseph Grew
    c. Major James F. Hollingsworth

A. David Bruce. Grew was U.S. ambassador to Japan in 1941; Hollingsworth, of the 67th Armored Regiment, was wounded in a heroic tank charge crossing the Elbe on the road to Berlin.

Q. Identify the head of the political arm of the Gaullist Resistance in Paris in 1944.

    a. Claude Guy
    b. André Tollet
    c. Alexandre Parodi

A. Alexandre Parodi. Guy was de Gaulle's aide, and Tollet was head of the Comité Parisien de la Libération.

Q. Who commanded the 6th Parachute Regiment (German) in Normandy on D-Day?

    a. Baron von der Heydte
    b. Count Klaus Schenk von Stauffenberg
    c. A noncom, senior officer present

A. Baron von der Heydte.

Q. What was the size of the Soviet cavalry?

    a. Under 10,000
    b. just over 100,000
    c. 600,000

A. 600,000.

Q. Identify the first ground recaptured from the Germans in the war.

    a. Calais, France
    b. Siddi Barrani, Egypt
    c. Smolensk, U.S.S.R.

A. Smolensk, U.S.S.R., in August 1941.

Q. When did the U.S. seize Axis ships that were in American ports?

    a. March 1941, while the U.S. was neutral
    b. December 8, 1941, when war with Japan was declared
    c. After Germany declared war on the U.S.

A. While still officially neutral, the U.S. seized Axis ships in U.S. ports in March 1941.

FACT The first ship sunk as a result of German mines in the Thames estuary was a Japanese passenger ship, the *Terukuni Maru*, on November 21, 1939.

Q. How many Russian guns opened fire on April 16, 1945, as they began the attack on Berlin?

    a. 5,000
    b. 10,000
    c. 20,000

A. There were 20,000 guns in a bombardment never previously equaled on the Eastern Front. (The firepower and unleashed energy were so great they created a hot wind that howled through the forest, bent saplings and lifted small objects into the air.)

Q. Hitler's order to destroy industries, communications and transportation that he feared were in jeopardy of falling into Allied or Russian hands was known as the:

    a. Denial Decree
    b. Nero Decree
    c. Phoenix Decree

A. Issued on March 19, 1945, as the U.S. 70th Division crossed the Saar River, the order was known as the Nero Decree because it resembled the order for the destruction of Rome by the infamous emperor.

Q. Identify the last U.S. airfield to be captured by the Japanese.

    a. Laohokow, China, March 1945
    b. Ormoc Bay, Philippines, 1942
    c. Kunming, China, 1943

A. Laohokow, China, near the end of March 1945. The U.S. Fourteenth Air Force destroyed anything of value prior to withdrawing, to deny Japanese use of the base.

Q. Which airborne operation was the largest of the war?

    a. German drop on Crete
    b. Allied drops in Operation Market Garden (Holland)
    c. Allied drops on Wesel

A. The British 6th and the U.S. 17th paratrooper drops on Wesel, March 24, 1945, which required approximately 40,000 paratroopers and just over 5,050 planes.

Q. When did the first V-2 bombs fall on London?

    a. October 10, 1943
    b. September 8, 1944
    c. January 1, 1945

A. September 8, 1944, in West London.

Q. When did Germany launch the last V-2 bomb against Great Britain?

    a. January 1945
    b. March 1945
    c. May 1, 1945

A. March 27, 1945. More than 2,850 people died from the bombs during their nearly seven months of terror, and another 6,000 sustained serious injuries.

Q. What was the percentage of U.S. Marine casualties during the initial assaults on Mount Suribachi, Iwo Jima?

    a. 10 to 20 percent
    b. 20 to 30 percent
    c. 40 to 50 percent

A. With progress measured in yards, as on Peleliu, and with half of their armored vehicles knocked out of action, the Marines sustained 20 to 30 percent casualties on February 19–20, 1945.

Q. When did the first U.S. Navy vessels return to action in Manila Bay after being driven out by the Japanese in 1942?

    a. 1943
    b. 1944
    c. 1945

A. Not until February 14, 1945, when PT boats began night reconnaissance missions.

FACT The Molotov cocktail, a popular and easily made explosive, got its name from the Finns, who used them extensively against the Russians in the winter of 1939–40.

Q. Who said, "The destruction of Dresden remains a serious query against the conduct of Allied bombing"?

    a. Franco of Spain
    b. Goering of Germany
    c. Churchill of Great Britain

A. The British Prime Minister, Winston Churchill, in commenting on what is considered the most devastating incendiary raid (February 13–14, 1945) of the war. More than 100,000 people were killed by the U.S. and British bombers.

Q. When did Hitler make his last radio broadcast of the war?

    a. One week after D-Day, June 1944
    b. January 30, 1945
    c. Two weeks before he died

A. On the twelfth anniversary of his taking control of Germany, January 30, 1945. He made his last appearance in public on March 20, when he presented medals to Hitler Youth who had performed with merit in combat.

Q. What was the relationship of casualties between the U.S. 77th Division and the Japanese troops involved in the battle on Leyte between December 20 and 31, 1944?

    a. 10,006 Japanese vs. 520 U.S.
    b. 3,107 Japanese vs. 302 U.S.
    c. 5,779 Japanese vs. 17 U.S.

A. It was 5,779 Japanese vs. 17 U.S.

Q. Name the island that was captured to open the way to Antwerp, and identify the Allied nation's troops that did it.

The island was:	The troops were:
a. Water Island	a. Canadian
b. Walter Island	b. Polish
c. Walcheren Island	c. French

A. The Canadian First Army, on November 8, 1944, captured Walcheren Island.

Q. Identify the site of the last Allied air raid of the war in Europe.

    a. Kiel
    b. Berlin
    c. Nuremberg

A. Royal Air Force Mosquitoes bombed Kiel on May 2, 1945, the last attack in Europe by bombers.

Q. When did Nazi Propaganda Minister Joseph Goebbels become Reich Minister of War?

    a. 1942
    b. 1943
    c. 1944

A. On July 25, 1944.

Q. Which army was first to cause Germany to fight on soil Germany had held prior to the war?

    a. Russia
    b. United States
    c. Great Britain

A. The Soviets engaged the Germans on the East Prussian border at the Sesupe River on August 17, 1944.

Q. What Continental European city was the target for the only long-range Luftwaffe air attack in the war?

    a. Brussels
    b. Amsterdam
    c. Eindhoven

A. Eindhoven, on September 19, 1944, when approximately 100 bombers raided.

FACT   When Adolf Hitler was told that France and Britain had declared war on Germany as a result of the invasion of Poland, the Fuehrer slumped in his chair and was silent for a few moments. Then, looking up at the generals around him, he asked, "Well . . . what do we do now?"

Q. Identify the general who led U.S. troops back to the Philippines on October 20, 1944.

    a. MacArthur
    b. Krueger
    c. Eichelberger

A. Lieutenant General Walter Krueger and the U.S. Sixth Army landed on the east coast of Leyte, establishing two beachheads. Four hours after the landing General MacArthur came ashore. He had indeed returned.

Q. Which naval battle is considered the greatest in history?

    a. Midway
    b. Leyte Gulf
    c. Coral Sea

A. The Battle of Leyte Gulf. The Japanese lost thirty-four ships, including four aircraft carriers and three battleships. The U.S. lost six ships, including one light aircraft carrier (*Princeton*) and two escort carriers (*Gambier Bay* and *St. Lo*).

Q. During the attack on Pearl Harbor, what was the first target hit by a Japanese bomb?

    a. Ford Island
    b. Hickham Field
    c. Battleship Row

A. Ford Island.

Q. Where was Japanese Admiral Yamamoto during the attack on Pearl Harbor?

    a. Tokyo
    b. With the attack force off Hawaii
    c. Aboard his flagship, *Nagato*, in Japanese waters.

A. He was aboard the *Nagato*.

Q. Identify the first Japanese aircraft carrier sunk by the U.S. in the war.

  a. *Shoho*
  b. *Shokaku*
  c. *Zuikaku*

A. The *Shoho*, during the Battle of the Coral Sea.

Q. Which type of ship was the largest lost by the U.S. in the battle for Okinawa?

  a. Destroyer
  b. Light cruiser
  c. Heavy cruiser
  d. Escort carrier
  e. Fleet carrier

A. Of the thirty-six ships lost, none was larger than a destroyer. The Japanese lost just under 200 ships of various sizes, up to the world's largest battleship, the *Yamato*.

Q. Where and when was Heinrich Himmler captured?

  a. Berlin, May 1945
  b. Bavaria, June 1945
  c. Bremervorde, May 1945

A. In Bremervorde by the British on May 21, 1945, while using false identity papers. He escaped justice by committing suicide while in captivity two days later at Lüneburg.

Q. Which one of the following countries stated it would be a non-belligerent on September 2, the day after war began in 1939?

  a. Italy
  b. Soviet Union
  c. Japan

A. Benito Mussolini made the declaration for Italy.

FACT The first planned bombing of Berlin by the Russians, on August 8, 1941, resulted in failure. Five planes on the mission could do nothing more than bomb a section of railroad on the outskirts of the city. Two planes were downed by German antiaircraft fire.

Q. With whom did France sign an armistice on the day that the Pétain government set up its headquarters in Vichy, June 24, 1940?

    a. Russia
    b. Germany
    c. Italy

A. The Italians. The document was signed in Rome.

Q. Identify the Norwegian King who fled to England on May 5, 1940.

    a. King Oscar III
    b. King Haakon VII
    c. King Erich V

A. King Haakon VII. The German invasion of his country had begun less than a month earlier, but despite strong Norwegian resistance, the monarch was advised to leave. Belgian King Leopold III, who remained in his country, became a German prisoner on May 28.

Q. Who conceived the idea for Radio Werewolf, the propaganda broadcasts intended to encourage last-ditch resistance in Germany?

    a. Hitler
    b. Himmler
    c. Goebbels

A. Joseph Goebbels. The program made its broadcasting debut on April 1, 1945, and was responsible for the slogan that lived through the cold war years into the 1950s: *Besser tot als rot,* which translates to "Better dead than Red."

Q. Who said, "I made a mistake and I shall pay for it, if my life can still serve as payment"?

    a. Benito Mussolini
    b. Erwin Rommel
    c. Isoroku Yamamoto

A. Mussolini, not very long before he died.

Q. The Japanese code name for the attack on Pearl Harbor was:

    a. Operation A
    b. Operation P
    c. Operation Z

A. In a discussion with his chief of staff in December 1940, Admiral Isoroku Yamamoto used the code name Operation Z for the possible attack on Pearl Harbor.

U.S. Army Photo

Q. Who said: "That is the biggest fool thing we have ever done. The bomb will never go off" in remarks concerning the atom bomb:

    a. Admiral King, USN
    b. General Arnold, USAF
    c. Admiral Leahy, USN

A. President Trumen's Chief of Staff, Admiral William Leahy, during a conversation with the President in 1945. In photo above, King, Arnold and Leahy check a wall map during a Joint Chiefs of Staff meeting.

Code Names

Q. Which American plane was known as the Flying Prostitute and why?

A. The Martin Marauder, a medium weight bomber, was known as the Flying Prostitute because it had no visible means of support. It was also called the Widow Maker for a time after it began service in 1942 because it was said to be unsafe.

Q. What was the code name for the breakout at St. Lo, Normandy?

A. Cobra.

Q. Which American unit was called the Rag-Tag Circus?

A. Because of the varied collection of enemy, civilian and other vehicles they used, the U.S. 83rd Infantry Division became known as the Rag-Tag Circus. Major General Robert C. Macon was the commander.

Q. What was the American equivalent of British Ultra called?

A. Magic.

Q. Who was Cicero?

A. A German agent who worked as a valet at the British Embassy in Turkey. Among other information he passed on was the meaning of the code name Operation Overload—the invasion of Europe. His name was Elyesa Bazna.

Q. What did the British call the DC-3?

A. The British and the Allied air forces in general termed the DC-3 and its modified versions—the C-47 and C-53—the Dakota.

Q. What was Operation Bolero?

A. The transfer of U.S. troops from America to England.

Q. Who was Iva D'Aquino?

A. Tokyo Rose. An American born to Japanese parents, she broadcast propaganda to American forces on behalf of Japan.

Q. Who was irreverently known as the Berlin Bitch by Allied troops in Europe?

A. Germany's answer to Tokyo Rose, Axis Sally.

Q. What was the code name for the Allied amphibious assault on the French Riviera?

A. Operation Anvil-Dragoon. Originally called Anvil, it was changed to Dragoon by the time of the actual invasion.

Q. Who was Lord Haw-Haw?

A. William Joyce, who was executed by the British for his radio broadcasts from Germany during the war.

Q. Who was known throughout Germany as the Voice of the High Command?

A. Lieutenant General Kurt Dittmar, a Wehrmacht officer who broadcast the latest news from the fronts during the war. He surrendered to the U.S. 30th Infantry at Magdeburg by making his way across the Elbe on April 23, 1945. (Dittmar told U.S. intelligence two things: the National Redoubt was a myth and Hitler was still in Berlin.)

Q. Who was Colonel Britain?

A. Douglas Ritchie, who was introduced at the end of BBC news as the voice of Supreme Headquarters, Allied Expeditionary Force. Remember those famous lines: "Our messages for our friends in occupied France tonight are . . ."?

Q. What was Winston Churchill's code name?

A. Colonel Warden.

Q. Who was Colonel Valerio?

A. Italian partisan commander Walter Audisio, the man who read the death sentence to Mussolini and ordered him and his mistress shot.

Q. Who was Colonel Rol?

A. Henry Tanguy, the communist leader in the Resistance in Paris.

Q. Who was named the Spy of the Century?

A. General Reinhard Gehlen, the man in charge of the German Army's intelligence and espionage network in the East. He later worked for the U.S. Army, the CIA and West Germany's espionage organization, the BND.

Q. What was the White Death?

A. The Finnish ski troops who in their white uniforms inflicted heavy casualties on the invading Soviets and nearly drove them out after the Russian attack on November 30, 1939.

Q. Who was Grofaz? (The term is an abbreviation for *grosster Feldherr aller Zeiten,* which means the greatest general of all time.)

A. Never as fond of their Fuehrer as people in other parts of Germany, the name Grofaz was sarcastically used by Berliners when speaking of Hitler.

Q. What was the Hooligan Navy?

A. The U.S. Coastal Picket Patrol. Organized in May 1942, it consisted of auxiliary yachts and motorboats under 100 feet in length. The civilian owners were often skippers who could not pass Navy qualifying exams. They were armed with small guns and depth charges to hunt U-boats. By February 1943 there were 550 of them, but they failed to make any "kills."

Q. What was General Patton's Navy?

A. The ships under Admiral H. Kent Hewitt that aided Patton with his "leapfrog" techniques along the coast of Sicily. Used to land his troops at points along the coast and to transport supplies, they helped Patton beat Monty to Messina.

Q. What was the U.S. Mystery ship project?

A. Heavily armed vessels disguised as peaceful merchantmen. Also known as the Q ship project, it accomplished nothing of significance and cost the lives of approximately one quarter of the sailors who volunteered. The ships were copied from those used for this purpose in World War I.

Q. What was the Schwarze Kapelle (Black Orchestra)?

A. The group of Germans, including Abwehr chief Admiral Wilhelm Canaris, that worked to overthrow Hitler and the Nazis.

Q. What was the Red Orchestra?

A. The Soviet spy ring active in Berlin during the war. The Luftwaffe squads that hunted for secret radio transmissions used the term "orchestra" to mean transmitter.

Q. What were the WASPS?

A. Nearly 2,000 American women who piloted every kind of plane the U.S. could produce, from Mustangs to B-29s, generally on delivery or ferry missions, between 1942 and 1944. Almost all of these women were experienced civilian pilots with more prewar flying hours to their credit than their male counterparts.

Q. What did the initials WAVES stand for?

A. Women Appointed for Voluntary Emergency Service, a branch of the U.S. Navy.

Q. What were the U.S. Women's Coast Guard Reserve members known as? Why?

A. They were the SPARS, from the motto of the U.S. Coast Guard— *Semper Paratus*—always ready.

Q. Which U.S. aircraft carrier was known as the Fighting Lady?

A. The U.S.S. *Yorktown,* also known as the Lucky Y because despite all the action she saw she received only one hit from the enemy.

Q. What ship was known as the Evil I?

A. Because of her ability to be in the way of Japanese torpedoes and bombs all too frequently, the U.S. aircraft carrier *Intrepid* had the nickname.

Q. What was the nickname of the battleship U.S.S. *Missouri?*

A. Mighty Mo.

Q. Which U.S. destroyer in the Pacific was nicknamed G. Q. Johnny?

A. The U.S.S. *Johnston,* because of the numerous general quarters alerts in combat.

Q. What was the bill in the U.S. Congress with the official designation of HR-1776 commonly known as?

A. Despite the patriotic designation, bill HR-1776 was better known as Lend-Lease.

Q. What was the Red Ball Highway?

A. The route, non-stop, heading northeast, that the seemingly endless convoy of U.S. Army supply trucks rolled along on to the Rhine and the Western Front. The trucks themselves were called the Red Ball Express.

Q. What was the Tokyo Express?

A. The name U.S Marines applied to the Japanese ships coming through the Slot in the Solomon Islands.

Q. What was the Caesar Line?

A. The German defense line protecting Rome.

Q. What were Rommel's asparagus?

A. Poles about six to twelve inches in diameter and eight to twelve feet long, approximately seventy-five feet apart. They were intended to deny the Allied airborne troops good landing zones during D-Day.

Q. Who was Smasher Karl?

A. Wehrmacht Lieutenant General Karl Weidling, who Hitler once ordered shot and then appointed commandant of Berlin in April 1945. On May 2, 1945, Weidling surrendered Berlin to the Russians.

Q. What was kickapoo joy juice?

A. The name GI's gave to the unusual alcoholic drink they managed to make during the campaign in Italy. (In the Pacific just about anything U.S. servicemen managed to brew was dubbed jungle juice.)

Q. Which branch of the U.S. military was known as the Silent Service?

A. The Navy's submarine fleet.

Q. What and when was Big Week?

A. February 19 to 25, 1944, when the Allies had over 6,000 bombers pounding at Germany. The Luftwaffe lost over 450 planes trying to stop the raids.

Q. During the campaign in North Africa what was known as Black Saturday?

A. June 13, 1942, Rommel's ambush of 300 British tanks under the command of General Sir Neil Ritchie. The Desert Fox destroyed 230 of them.

Q. What was the name of the RAF plan to employ all available aircraft against the Luftwaffe as it approached Coventry?

A. Operation Cold Douche, which had little success.

Q. What was the German Kondor Mission?

A. Their intelligence operation in Cairo, Egypt.

Q. What was P. C. Bruno?

A. The code name for the French cryptographic service prior to occupation by the Germans. It functioned from the Chàteau Vignolle approximately twenty-five miles from Paris.

Q. By what name did Hitler and the German High Command identify the counteroffensive in the Ardennes Forest that the Allies called the Battle of the Bulge?

A. Watch on the Rhine.

Q. What was Eagle Day?

A. The 1,000-bomber, 700-fighter-plane raid on London on August 15, 1940, by the Luftwaffe.

FACT Italian dictator Benito Mussolini is credited with creating the term Axis as it applied to that group of nations in the war. On November 1, 1936, after reaching a secret agreement with Hitler, Mussolini gave a speech in Milan in which he said, "The vertical line between Rome and Berlin is not a partition but rather an axis round which all European states animated by the will to collaboration and peace can also collaborate."

Q. What was the Battalion of Heaven?

A. Chasseurs Parachutistes, the 4th SAS Regiment, the French unit that employed airborne drops behind German lines in Europe after the Normandy invasion. They practiced guerrilla and commando-style tactics.

Q. What was the Cactus Air Force?

A. The name adopted by the Navy and Marine pilots operating out of Henderson Field during the Guadalcanal campaign.

Q. Who were the Martians?

A. The Allied personnel from SHAEF in London who were responsible for the evaluation of intelligence.

Q. Which plane did Allied bomber crews nickname Little Friend?

A. The longest-range fighter escort in action during the war, the Mustang.

Q. What was the name of the Lockheed Lodestar that carried De Gaulle back to France?

A. The *France,* piloted by Colonel Lionel de Marmier.

Q. What was General Hideki Tojo's nickname?

A. Razor Brain.

Q. Who was nicknamed the Fuehrer's Brown Eminence?

A. Martin Bormann, who owned and wore only brown boots rather than the black boots that others in Hitler's circle were fond of.

Q. Which American general did the Chinese affectionately call Old Leather Face?

A. General Claire Chennault.

Q. Identify the British General nicknamed Jumbo.

A. General Sir Henry Wilson.

Q. Which American general was known as Vinegar Joe?

A. General Joseph Stilwell.

Q. What was FDR's code name?

A. Victor. The American President was also known as Admiral Q in certain messages. President Truman was code-named Kilting.

Q. Who was Popski?

A. Lieutenant Colonel Vladimir Peniakoff, the British commando who became a legend from Africa to Italy leading Popski's Private Army.

Q. Which Allied general was known as the Impatient Lion?

A. Jacques Leclerc of the Free French.

Q. Identify the Italian general nicknamed Electric Whiskers by his own troops.

A. Bergonzoli, who was captured by the British in the African campaign. The name referred to his red beard.

Q. Who was known as the Father of the Royal Air Force?

A. Air Marshal Lord Hugh Trenchard, who developed the RAF between 1919 and 1929. He came out of retirement in 1939 at age sixty-six.

Q. Who is known as the Father of the Atomic Bomb?

A. Dr. Robert Oppenheimer. He was denied security clearance nine years after he headed the team that developed the bomb.

Q. What name and rank did the British give to the body deposited off the Spanish coast in the hopes the Axis would think it was a dead secret courier?

A. Major Martin. The body had an attaché case replete with "secret" communications indicating the British would land in Greece or Sardinia instead of Sicily. The Germans believed the ploy, but the Italians were not convinced.

FACT In an effort to thwart Allied bombing raids on Germany, reproductions of Berlin, Hamburg and other areas were built near enough to the actual sites to confuse aircraft. However, they were far enough away to provide safety for the inhabitants. There were no less than five copies of Berlin alone sprinkled across the German landscape in giant scale.

Q. What were Flash and Thunder?

A. The passwords that were used by the 82nd Airborne in addition to tin toy snappers to identify friendly troops after the drop on Normandy.

Q. What was the real name of the Dutch Intelligence Service officer known as Captain Harry who jumped with the 82nd Airborne in Nijmegen, Holland?

A. Arie D. Bestebreurtje. Actually he participated in several missions with U.S. forces, and was involved in the planning for the airborne drop on Tempelhof Airport in Berlin.

Q. Who were known as the Golden Pheasants?

A. The select group of Nazi officials who were permitted to wear the gilded swastika.

Q. To whom did FDR refer as Uncle Joe?

A. Joseph Stalin. However, the Allied code name for Stalin was Glyptic.

Q. What was the name of Hitler's private train?

A. Amerika.

Q. What was the name of the private train Reichsfuehrer Heinrich Himmler used?

A. Steiermark.

Q. What period of the war did German submariners call the Happy Time?

A. The summer and fall of 1940, when they were sinking an average of eight ships per U-boat per month.

Q. What did Rommel call Devil's Gardens?

A. The extensive German minefields at El Alamein.

FACT   The U.S. Selective Service Act, which had been law for one year in 1940, was continued in 1941 by a margin of one vote in the House of Representatives, less than four months before the attack on Pearl Harbor.

U.S. Army Photo

Q. What was the real name of French General Jacques Leclerc?

A. Philippe François Marie Leclerc de Hautecloque. After joining the Free
French he changed it to protect his family still in France. In photo above
Leclerc (right), as commander of the French 2nd Armored Division, is
congratulated by U.S. General Walton H. Walker on the beach at Normandy on July 31, 1944.

Q. What were the Stalin Organs?

A. Rockets fired from launchers with an ear-splitting screech. Their Russian name was Katushkas. Fired at night, they produced a long white trail.

Q. What was the Sitzkrieg?

A. The period from September 1939, when war was declared on Germany, and the start of actual fighting by Britain and France early in 1940. In the English-speaking world it was called the phony war.

Q. What does blitzkrieg mean?

A. Lightning war, which was popularized after the rapid German advance on Poland in 1939.

Q. What significance did Wagner's "Twilight of the Gods" have for members of the Berlin Philharmonic Orchestra?

A. They knew that the night they were requested to play it would be the night Armament and War Production Minister Albert Speer had made arrangements for them to flee Berlin to the West rather than be captured by the Russians.

Q. What was a Fuehrer Paket?

A. The packages of food Hitler gave as gifts to important military personnel he summoned to his headquarters at Rastenburg.

Q. What was Hitler's dog named?

A. Blondie.

Q. What was Big B?

A. For the Eighth Air Force fliers who flew the missions, Berlin was Big B.

FACT   During the Battle of Britain Churchill sent the last seventy tanks on the island to British forces fighting in North Africa. He felt that if the situation in Great Britain got to a point where the tanks would be a crucial ingredient, the battle would already be lost. In justifying their movement to Egypt he said: "I have not become the King's First Minister to preside over the liquidation of the British Empire."

Q. What was the German code name for the operation that involved penetrating U.S. lines with English-speaking troops in U.S. uniforms?

A. Greif. It was under the command of SS commando Otto Skorzeny and intended for widespread use during the Battle of the Bulge.

Q. What was the German code name for the bombing of Coventry, England, on November 14–15, 1940?

A. Moonlight Sonata.

Q. The Allied scheme that involved the Man Who Never Was had two code names. What were they?

A. Mincemeat and Trojan Horse. Carried out in 1943, it was conceived to mislead the Germans about Allied invasion intentions in Italy.

Q. How did Churchill sign his correspondence with FDR?

A. Former Naval Person, which he seemed to delight in. Churchill had been in charge of the Admiralty at times during both World Wars.

Q. Which German general was nicknamed Unser Giftzwerg (our poison dwarf)?

A. Colonel General Gotthard Heinrici, the short, tough general ordered to hold the Russians on the Oder River as commander of Army Group Vistula. The name was used by those who liked him as a compliment and by those who disliked him, including Hitler, as derogatory.

Q. What was the Night of the Long Knives? When was it?

A. The changing of the guard for Hitler. On June 30, 1934, his SS murdered eighty-three members of the SA, his former personal army.

Q. What were the eight code names used for the subdivided sections of Omaha Beach on D-Day?

A. They were Easy Red, Fox Red, Fox Green, Charlie, Easy Green, Dog Green, Dog White and Dog Red.

Q. Which island did the Marines call the Killing Ground?

A. Tarawa.

Q. What battle was known as the Great Marianas Turkey Shoot?

A. The Battle of the Philippine Sea, June 19–21, 1944. So named by an aviator because U.S. forces destroyed 346 Japanese planes and two carriers. The U.S. lost thirty planes and no ships. It marked virtually the end of significant Japanese carrier opposition.

Q. What were the circumstances under which the following bulletin was transmitted by accident on June 4, two days before the D-Day invasion: "Urgent Press Associated NYK Flash Eisenhower's HQ announced Allied landings in France"?

A. An Associated Press teletype operator had been trying to build up transmitting speed and the perforated tape was somehow mixed in with "live" tape.

Q. What did the coded message Ham and Jam mean?

A. Sent by British 6th Airborne paratroopers, it was the message indicating that the unit had captured two vital bridges over the Caen Canal and Orne River.

Q. Which U.S. Army division was known as the Victory Division?

A. The 5th Armored Division.

Q. Name the U.S. division whose unusual tactics earned it the name Hell on Wheels.

A. The 2nd Armored, which confused the Germans from North Africa onward.

Q. Which division was known as the Screaming Eagles?

A. The 101st Airborne Division.

FACT Boise City, Oklahoma, holds the distinction of being the only mainland U.S. town bombed during the war. However, the incident was not the result of Axis ability to penetrate U.S. defenses. A U.S. Air Force bomber on a training mission from Dalhart, Texas, knocked out the local Baptist church and another building—which were over forty miles from the target range. No casualties resulted in Boise City, but the future flight status of the pilot and crew were seriously questioned.

Q. What and when was Kristalnacht?

A. On November 10, 1938, a "spontaneous" anti-Jewish demonstration was staged because German diplomat Ernst von Rath had been assassinated by a Jew. Stores and shops were ruined, synagogues burned, Jews beaten and arrested.

Q. By what name did the Allied troops know the peaceful-looking seacoast area of Vierville?

A. Omaha Beach, Normandy.

Q. What were Ascension Day Rations?

A. The extra portions of food the German government issued to Berliners on April 20, 1945, Hitler's birthday. They were properly called crisis rations, and many Germans believed they had gotten the extra food because the government expected them to "ascend into heaven" before the Russians captured the city.

Q. Identify the code names of the three Paris transmitters used by the Resistance to communicate with the Allies.

A. Apollo Black, Montparnasse Black and Pleyel Violet.

Q. What was the Eagle's Nest?

A. Hitler's mountain retreat at Berchtesgaden.

Q. What was the name of Hitler's headquarters at Rastenburg?

A. Wolf's Lair.

Q. What was the Little Red School House?

A. SHAEF (Supreme Headquarters Allied Expeditionary Force) in Reims, France.

Q. Who were the Devils in Skirts?

A. The British 51st Highland Division.

Q. Identify the U.S. division known as the Railsplitters?

A. The 84th Infantry Division.

Q. What was the U.S. 4th Infantry Division called?

A. The Ivy Division.

Q. Which U.S. division was called the Blue and Gray?

A. The 29th Division.

Q. What were the German Goliaths?

A. Miniature robot tanks with over a half ton of explosives. Guided by remote control, they were intended to be sent among Allied troops and vehicles and set off.

Q. What was the name of the ersatz coffee Parisians turned to during the occupation?

A. Café National.

Q. What was Paname?

A. A French slang word for Paris. It first came into general use after Edith Piaf sang it in a song prior to the war.

Q. What was the official name of General de Gaulle's Free French provisional government?

A. Comité Français de Libération Nationale (CFLN).

Q. What was the Red Plan the French underground was to execute upon hearing the BBC message "The dice are on the table"?

A. The cutting of all phone and communication lines in advance of D-Day.

Q. What was General von Choltitz's headquarters in Paris code-named at the time of the city's liberation?

A. Located in the Hotel Meurice on the Rue de Rivoli across from Tuileries Gardens, the headquarters code name was Hypnose.

Q. What are the three code names used for the forty-, thirty-, and nine-ton bridges the Allies constructed near Monte Cassino, Italy?

A. The forty-ton bridge was Amazon, the thirty-ton was Blackwater and the nine-ton was Congo. They crossed the Rapido River.

Q. What were the German Werewolves?

A. Commando troops the Allies feared would operate from the National Redoubt after the end of hostilities. The name Werewolves was used by propaganda Minister Joseph Goebbels.

Q. What were the Chindits?

A. British Major General Orde Wingate's forces in the China-Burma-India theater. Chindit was a bastardization of the Burmese word for lion, *chinthe*. Wingate's Chindits successfully foiled the Japanese in their efforts to capture India.

Q. What was the popular name of the special American combat infantry team known as the Galahad Force that was commanded by Brigadier General Frank D. Merrill?

A. Merrill's Marauders.

Q. When did the U.S. succeed in breaking the Japanese Purple code?

A. In September 1940. It enabled the U.S. to read the most confidential messages Tokyo sent to its diplomatic corps for more than fourteen months before the attack on Pearl Harbor.

Q. What was the Carpetbagger Squadron?

A. The Army Air Force unit that dropped arms and supplies to the Resistance fighters in the Fortress Europe. They flew over 300 missions from January 1943 to the end of the war in Europe.

Q. Which German aircraft was known as the Flaming Coffin?

A. The Heinkel He-177, Germany's only heavy bomber. About 1,000 were produced.

Q. Which British plane did the Germans nickname Stachelschwein (porcupine)?

A. The well-armed Short Sunderland Flying Boat, which had great success in anti-U-boat warfare.

FACT One of the most unusual devices for identification used by any nation was the employing of fireworks by the U.S. Regimental Combat Team during the North African invasion. In an effort to convince the Vichy French at Oran that the invasion force was U.S., not British, the Americans shot firework bombs that exploded into 100-foot-wide U.S. flags overhead. (The French were hostile to the British, who had recently attacked their fleet in the harbor.) The U.S. troops also used loudspeakers which identified the Americans as not being British troops.

Q. What was Plan Green?

A. The code name the French underground gave to the operation to smash German railroad traffic.

Q. What was the German code name for the invasion of Russia?

A. Barbarossa.

Q. What was Operation Eclipse?

A. The Allied plan for the occupation of Berlin, including the sectors that were to be occupied by the major powers. Prior to November 1944, it was also known as Operation Rankin, Case C and Operation Talisman.

Q. What was Operation Punishment?

A. When the Yugoslavs overthrew their government and repudiated the treaty of "alliance" with Germany in the spring of 1941, Hitler ordered the savage bombing of Belgrade, killing 17,000, which he termed Operation Punishment.

Q. What was the German and Italian code name for the attack on Malta?

A. Operation Herkules. It was called off when the Germans succeeded in taking Tobruk. The Malta-bound troops were given to Rommel.

Q. What was the German code name for the planned invasion of England?

A. Operation Sea Lion.

Q. What was Operation Roundup?

A. The code name for the 1943 Allied plan to invade Europe.

Q. What was Plan Jael?

A. The operation to convince the Germans that the Normandy D-Day landings would take place elsewhere. Jael was an Old Testament woman accused of treachery. It was renamed Plan Bodyguard after a quote that appears elsewhere in this book.

Q. What was Operation Fortitude?

A. The code name for the cover plan for the D-Day invasion to convince the Germans it would take place at Pas de Calais. This was different from Plan Jael in that it indicated a specific area.

Q. What was Operation Gambit?

A. The British submarine mission that went in close to the French coastline in advance of the Normandy landings in June 1944. They functioned as navigational markers for British and Canadian troops. Two subs, X-20 and X-23, were involved.

Q. What was the code name for the Allied invasion of North Africa?

A. Operation Torch.

Q. What was Operation Jubilant?

A. The plan for Allied airborne drops on prisoner of war camps as the Allies pushed deeper into Germany.

Q. What was the code name for the proposed Allied airborne attack on the German naval base at Kiel?

A. Operation Eruption.

Q. What was the German code name for the plan to take Moscow?

A. Typhoon.

Q. What was the code name for the plan that would have dropped U.S. airborne troops on the trio of airfields around Rome?

A. Giant II, which was never employed.

Q. What was Operation Yellow?

A. German's actions against Belgium, Holland and Luxembourg.

Q. What was Operation Puakenschlag?

A. Operation Paukenschlag (roll of the drums) was the name for U-boat assaults on U.S. coastal and Caribbean shipping from January to July 1942.

Q. What was the naval portion of the D-Day invasion code-named?

A. Operation Neptune.

FACT The most destructive single bombing mission of the war took place March 9–10, 1945, when 334 B-29s raided Tokyo and left 1.25 million people homeless. This raid caused more damage than the atom bombs on Hiroshima and Nagasaki.

Q. Which German commander was called Smiling Albert by the Allies?

A. Field Marshal Albert Kesselring, shown here while being held as a witness by the Allies during the Nuremberg war crimes trials in November 1945.

Q. What was A-Day?

A. The Allied code name for the beginning of the assault on Berlin, April 16, 1945.

Q. What was the code name for the evacuation at Dunkirk?

A. Operation Dynamo.

Q. What was the German code word that indicated the Russian attack on Berlin?

A. Clausewitz.

Q. What was Operation Beggar?

A. The plan to drop guns and supplies to the Resistance fighters in Paris in August 1944. Instead, the planes brought food and coal to the French city on August 26 after it was liberated.

Q. What was Operation Diadem?

A. The liberation of Rome.

Q. What was the Allied code name for Great Britain?

A. Wildflower.

Q. Which Allied air operation was known as Soapsuds?

A. The bombing of Ploesti, Rumania, on August 1, 1943.

Q. Operation Venerable, the Allied plan to open the French port of Bordeaux, was known earlier by what name?

A. Operation Independence.

Q. What was the England-to-Russia air shuttle bombing known as?

A. Operation Frantic.

Q. What was Fanfare?

A. The Allied code name for all operations in the Mediterranean.

Q. What was the code name for the U.S. invasion and liberation of the Philippines?

A. Excelsior.

Q. What was the Allied operation to paralyze the German transportation system called?

A. Operation Clarion.

Q. What was Operation Baytown?

A. The invasion of Italy by the British Eighth Army via Messina.

Q. What was Fat Boy?

A. The code name for the plutonium atom bomb dropped on Nagasaki.

Q. What was Little Boy?

A. The code name for the uranium atom bomb dropped on Hiroshima.

Q. What was Operation Crossbow?

A. The code name for Allied air raids against Germany's V-1 launch sites.

Q. What was the code name for the deceptive operation to make the Germans believe the Allies had an invasion fleet off the coast of Boulogne on D-Day?

A. Operation Glimmer.

Q. What was the code name for the Allied raid on Dieppe, France, in 1942?

A. Operation Jubilee. However, it was originally called Operation Rutter.

Q. What were Zeal, Thumb and Pearl often used as code names for?

A. Information from the Enigma code machines. Rather than risk using the code name Ultra for such information passed on to field commanders below the rank of commanding generals, the British used a series of code names.

Q. What was the English-French operation against Dakar in 1940 code named?

A. Menace.

Q. What was the Garibaldi Partisan Division?

A. Two Italian divisions that fought along with Tito's troops against the Germans in Yugoslavia after Italy declared war on Germany.

Q. What was Piccolo Peak?

A. A hill in the battle for Salerno that General Mark Clark had assigned a regimental band to defend. The name came *after* the troops were assigned.

Q. What was the code name for the unsuccessful 1943 attempt to kill Hitler by placing a bomb in his plane?

A. Flash. Many of the same German officers who would later take part in the July 20, 1944, attempt were involved in this.

Q. What was the German generals' code name for the plot to kill Hitler in 1944?

A. Operation Valkyrie, which failed on July 20, 1944.

Q. What was the code word the German generals in the plot to kill Hitler awaited as news that the mission had succeeded?

Q. Ubung. Because it was sent out prematurely, several conspirators quickly ordered SS, Gestapo and other Nazis in their area arrested. Their fast action earned them death sentences.

Q. What was the code name for the plan to capture or kill Field Marshal Rommel in France in 1944?

A. Operation Gaff.

Q. What was called a great crusade?

A. The Allied efforts to wrest Europe from the grasp of the Nazis. Dwight Eisenhower popularized it.

Q. What was Special Operations Executive?

A. The British organization, established in 1940, that organized subversion and sabotage in German-occupied countries.

Q. What was known as the Gibraltar of the South Pacific?

A. Rabaul on New Britain island.

FACT The United States was asked to join the Tripartite Pact alliance with Japan, Germany and Italy "in the spirit of the new order... in which ... the natural geographic divisions of the earth established in complementary fashion" would be the goal. Japan extended the invitation on October 13, 1940.

Q. What did Gustav mean in the German code with regard to Tempelhof Airport?

A. It was the warning that Allied planes were heading for the airport.

Q. What was Duroc?

A. Named for one of Napoleon's generals, Duroc was the underground control center for the French Resistance in August 1944. It covered approximately 300 miles of tunnels and sewers of the metro system and sanitation department.

Q. What was Exchange 500?

A. The largest telephone and communications center in Germany, linking Hitler, OKW and other bases with field commanders in Germany and conquered territories.

Q. What was PLUTO?

A. Pipe Line Under the Ocean, the trans-Channel fuel transport line from England to France that fed the Allied supply lines after the Normandy invasion.

Q. What were the artificial harbors constructed for Operation Overlord called?

A. Mulberry.

Q. What was the Manhattan Engineer District?

A. Established in August 1942, it was the name of the U.S. project that worked to build the atom bomb. It was also known as the Manhattan Project.

Q. What were Millennium and Millennium II?

A. Code names for the thousand-bomber raids on Cologne and Bremen.

Q. What were Maybach I and Maybach II?

A. Mayback I was the headquarters of OKH, the German Army High Command. Maybach II was the German OKW, Armed Forces High Command, and Hitler's headquarters, located in Zossen.

Q. What were Bangalore torpedoes?

A. Devices used to destroy barbwire obstacles, usually lengths of pipe filled with explosives.

Q. What is a MOMP?

A. Navy lingo for Mid Ocean Meeting Point.

Q. What is Condition Zed?

A. Complete watertight integrity on a ship.

Q. In U.S. jargon what does SOPA stand for?

A. Senior Officer Present Afloat.

Q. What was AMGOT?

A. Allied Military Government of Occupied Territories.

Q. What was Eisenhower's Circus Wagon?

A. The trailer he used in England during the planning for D-Day.

Q. Who was Jade Amicol?

A. Colonel Claude Ollivier, chief of the British Intelligence Service in occupied France.

Q. What did membership in the Caterpillar Club say about a pilot?

A. That the American pilot had successfully bailed out of an aircraft. Possession of a parachute ripcord handle was considered proof.

Q. What weapon was known as the Earthquake bomb?

A. The ten-ton bombs in the Allied arsenal. The first one was dropped on Germany in March 1945.

Q. Who was General Bor?

A. General Tadeusz Komorovski, leader of the Polish underground in Warsaw, which began an aggressive campaign against the Germans on August 1, 1944, because they believed the Russians were about to arrive.

FACT The *Queen Mary*, with 10,000 U.S. troops aboard and en route to Great Britain, sliced the British cruiser *Curaçao* in half in October 1942. The *Curaçao* was escorting the *Queen*, which made a course correction but did not alert the warship. Casualties aboard the two halves of the cruiser were 338 killed. The *Queen*, fearing U-boats, did not stop to participate in rescue operations.

Q. What was the Night and Fog Decree?

A. An order, authorized by Hitler, to eliminate all persons considered a threat to German security throughout Fortress Europe. The eliminations, however, were to be conducted in a discreet manner whereby victims would simply disappear into the "night and fog," leaving no trace.

Q. What did the designation CV indicate with regard to U.S. aircraft carriers?

A. The *C* designated the ship as a carrier, while the *V* represented heavier than air, the aircraft on carriers. Thus the CV classification was for ships that were carriers of heavier-than-air planes.

Q. Identify the London hotel that became known as the Blitz Hotel.

A. Because it was the home away from home for numerous British and foreign dignitaries, monarchs, heads of state in exile and the leading newsmen from the U.S., the Savoy earned the name.

Q. Which U.S. air base was known as Cochran's Convent and why?

A. Avenger Field, near Sweetwater, Texas. It was the home of the Women's Air Force Service Pilots (WASP's) and the only all-female U.S. air base in history. The nickname was a lighthearted tribute to one of the two women responsible for female pilots having an opportunity to contribute their skills to the war, Jacqueline Cochrane. The other aviatrix who worked at putting women in the sky for the war effort was Nancy Harkness Love.

Q. What was the cipher used by U.S. military attachés during the war until it was compromised?

A. The Black Code, which had been copied by an Italian spy working in the U.S. Embassy in Rome in August 1944. Passed on to the Germans, it was "read" by the enemy for a full year before being changed.

FACT The U.S. submarine *Tullibee*, March 26, 1944, off Palau in the Carolines, fired two torpedoes at a Japanese transport. One of the torpedoes began a full circle and hit the submarine, sinking it. Only one crewman survived.

Messages
and Quotations

Q. Kilroy was here. Who said it? What did it mean?

A. James J. Kilroy, a rivet inspection checker at the Fore River Shipyard in Quincy, Massachusetts, wrote the legend next to work he checked rather than make small chalk marks that piece workers could erase and thereby hope to have counted twice. As a result, ships departed the yard with the words that would become an almost cult-slogan throughout the war. U.S. servicemen, amused at the legend, scratched, painted, wrote and carved "Kilroy was here" on thousands of buildings, monuments, vehicles and toilet walls.

Q. Who sent the historic message "Air Raid, Pearl Harbor—This is no drill"?

A. An unidentified caller contacted CINCPAC Headquarters by phone prior to 7:58 A.M. on December 7, 1941, with the message "Enemy air raid, not drill." Rear Admiral Patrick Bellinger sent out at 7:58 from Ford Island: "Air Raid, Pearl Harbor—This is no drill." At 8 A.M. Commander Vincent Murphy at CINCPAC Headquarters sent out "Air raid on Pearl Harbor. This is no drill." Bellinger is credited with the message picked up by a West Coast radio station and carried across the country to Washington.

Q. Who gave the signal "All ships in harbor sortie"? Where? When?

A. Rear Admiral William R. Furlong aboard the minelayer *Ogala* almost at the same moment someone telephoned CINCPAC headquarters "Enemy air raid, not drill." Both of these alerts went out from Pearl Harbor minutes before Admiral Bellinger's historic message.

Q. Who said, "Believe me, Lang, the first twenty-four hours of the invasion will be decisive . . . for the Allies as well as Germany it will be the longest day"?

A. Field Marshal Erwin Rommel to an aide in April 1944.

Q. "Uncommon valor was a common virtue." Who said it, where and when?

A. Admiral Chester Nimitz, after the capture of Iwo Jima.

Q. Who said, "Show this gentleman out through the back door"?

A. Soviet Commissar for Foreign Affairs Vyacheslav Molotov to his secretary after receiving the German declaration of war from Count Werner von der Schulenburg. Hostilities had already begun.

Q. Who said, "Pearl Harbor will never be attacked from the air"?

A. United States Admiral Charles H. McMorris, on December 3, 1941, four days before it happened.

Q. Who said, "But, sir, I think we might be going a bridge too far"?

A. Lieutenant General Frederick Browning, deputy commander, First Allied Airborne Army, at the final conference at Montgomery's headquarters before Operation Market Garden, the drop on Holland.

Q. At whom did Hitler scream *"Brennt Paris?"* ("Is Paris burning?")?

A. His chief of staff, Generaloberst Alfred Jodl, on August 25, 1944. He continued: "Jodl, I want to know . . . is Paris burning? Is Paris burning right now, Jodl?"

Q. Who responded to the German surrender ultimatum with one word, "Nuts"? Where and when?

A. U.S. General Anthony Clement McAuliffe while acting commander of the 101st Airborne at Bastogne during the Battle of the Bulge in 1944.

Q. What was the American retort to the British quip "You Yanks are overpaid, oversexed and over here"?

A. "You're underpaid, undersexed and under Eisenhower."

Ullstein Photo

Q. Who called Hitler's Atlantic Wall a "figment of Hitler's cloud cuckoo land"?

A. The man who was once his favorite general, Field Marshal Erwin Rommel. He made the comment after inspecting it and seeing its numerous deficiencies. Rommel and other senior staff officers are seen above on May 29, 1944, eight days before the Normandy invasion began, on an inspection trip to the Atlantic Wall.

Q. Who said, "I'll put an end to the idea that a woman's body belongs to her ... the practice of abortion shall be exterminated with a strong hand"?

A. Adolf Hitler, in *Mein Kampf*. And he followed through by sentencing women who had abortions to hard labor. A second offense brought death. This only applied to Aryan women, however.

Q. Who claimed he had secured Peace in Our Time?

A. British Prime Minister Neville Chamberlain after visiting Hitler at the Munich Conference. Germany invaded Czechoslovakia less than six months later.

Q. To whom was the Cromwell quote "You have sat too long here for any good you have been doing. Depart, I say, and let us have done with you. In the name of God, go" repeated in 1940?

A. To British Prime Minister Neville Chamberlain in Parliament by Conservative member Leopold Amery. It signified the displeasure with the government's handling of the war up to that time. Two days later Chamberlain was out, Churchill in.

Q. East Wind, Rain—what did it mean?

A. This was the coded weather broadcast signal Japan may or may not have sent to its intelligence forces abroad to indicate that Japanese-U.S. relations were in danger. Along with similar codes it was intended for use between mid-November and December 7, 1941.

Q. What did "Climb Mount Niitaka" mean?

A. It was the coded message to the Japanese fleet on December 2, 1941, that irrevocably ordered the attack on Pearl Harbor.

FACT   The German Navy developed magnetic mines which remained on the sea floor and were activated by the magnetic field generated by a ship passing overhead. This was a great improvement over moored contact mines, which could be located by minesweepers, their cables cut and then destroyed by small arms fire. Britain overcame the magnetic mines through the use of an electric cable around ships' hulls, thereby countering the magnetic field.

Q. Who prepared the following message: "Our landings in the Cherbourg-Havre area have failed to gain a satisfactory foothold and I have withdrawn the troops.... If there is any blame or fault attached to the attempt, it is mine alone"?

A. General Dwight D. Eisenhower, Supreme Allied Commander. It was Ike's *"other"* message "that was never sent" in the event the Normandy invasion failed.

Q. Who said; "If I was commander of the Allied forces right now, I could finish off the war in fourteen days"?

A. Field Marshal Erwin Rommel on D-Day, June 6, 1944, as he raced back to his Army Group B from his home in Germany.

Q. What were the two messages that came over the transport ships' loudspeakers that most D-Day veterans still remember?

A. The command "Away all boats," and the Lord's Prayer.

Q. Who said; "Two kinds of people are staying on this beach, the dead and those who are going to die. Now let's get the hell out of here"?

A. Colonel George A. Taylor, the 16th Infantry Regiment's commanding officer, to men on Omaha Beach on D-Day.

Q. Who said; "I hope Vichy drives them back into the sea" when he was informed that the Allies had invaded North Africa?

A. General Charles de Gaulle, who had not been told of the planned invasion. (The United States did not recognize de Gaulle's position as head of the French provisional government but did recognize the Vichy government and had negotiated with Admiral Jean Darlan to eliminate resistance to the landings.)

Q. Who said, "There are only two rules of war. Never invade Russia. Never invade China"?

A. Field Marshal Sir Bernard Law Montgomery.

Q. Who said, "The last man who sees Hitler wins the game"?

A. Rommel to an aide when discussing the Fuehrer's ability to change his mind or make a decision.

Q. Who said; "There'll be no Dunkirk here"? Where?

A. British General L. J. Morshead, commander at Tobruk.

U.S. Army Photo

Q. Who said, "Compared to war, all other forms of human endeavor shrink to insignificance. God, how I love it"?

A. U.S. Army General George Patton, who also said, "Peace is going to be hell on me," in a letter to his wife. In the August 26, 1944, photo above, Patton confers with officers of the 5th Division, under his command, on the progress in crossing the Seine River in France.

Q. Who said, "Firing [General Sir Claude] Auchinleck was like killing a magnificent stag"?

A. Winston Churchill, after he fired Auchinleck as commander in North Africa.

Q. Who said, "Suppose my neighbor's home catches fire, and I have a length of garden hose . . ." about what?

A. FDR at a press conference prior to asking Congress to pass Lend-Lease.

Q. Who said, "All the same, a formidable people, a very great people . . . to have pushed this far"? About whom?

A. Charles de Gaulle, when visiting Moscow. The rest of the quote is "I don't speak of the Russians, I speak of the Germans."

Q. Who said the following about whom? "His ardor and daring inflicted grievous disasters upon us . . . a great general."

A. Winston Churchill about Erwin Rommel.

Q. Who said, "My Fuehrer, I congratulate you! Roosevelt is dead. It is written in the stars. The last half of April will be the turning point for us"?

A. Propaganda Minister Joseph Goebbels, on April 13, the day after Roosevelt died. Hitler would take his own life seventeen days later, and Goebbels and his wife and six children would be dead a day later.

Q. Who said, "The hand that held the dagger has struck it into the back of its neighbor"? About what?

A. FDR, commenting on Italy's entry into the war against the Allies on June 10, 1940, made the statement in a speech at the University of Virginia.

Q. Who said, "I only wish Herr Reichsmarschall, that we were issued similar razor blades!"—about what, to whom?

A. Rommel to Goering when the latter brushed off reports that the British were destroying Rommel's panzers with American shells. Goering said, "All the Americans can make are razor blades and refrigerators."

Q. Who said, "Praise the Lord and pass the ammunition," and when?

A. Chaplain Howell Forgy, aboard the *New Orleans* during the attack on Pearl Harbor, popularized the remark which, according to U.S.M.C. Major Louis E. Fagan was uttered in 1689 by the Reverend Dr. Walker during the defense of Londonderry from the forces of King James II.

Q. Who said, "I'm too old a bunny to get too excited about this"? About what?

A. General Hans von Salmuth, Commanding Officer of the German Fifteenth Army, when told that the second part of the coded message announcing the invasion of Europe had been intercepted. He continued to play bridge with other officers.

Q. Who said, "Hitler has missed the bus"?

A. British Prime Minister Chamberlain, commenting on the "phony war." The full quote was "After seven months of war I feel ten times as confident of victory as I did at the beginning. Hitler has missed the bus."

Q. Who said, "Berlin is no longer a military objective"?

A. Supreme Allied Commander Dwight D. Eisenhower, on April 14, 1945, when he announced that the Anglo-American drive toward Germany's capital would be halted. Some troops were only forty-five miles away.

Q. Who created the motto "The Fuehrer commands, we follow"?

A. Dr. Joseph Paul Goebbels, Germany's Propaganda Minister.

Q. "That Bohemian corporal, Hitler, usually decides against himself." Who said it?

A. Field Marshal Gerd von Rundstedt upon learning that Rommel, who was his junior, would be redesigning the anti-invasion defenses of the European coast—under orders from Hitler.

FACT The worst air raid on Paris came the day after liberation on August 26, 1944. Nearly 150 planes of the Luftwaffe bombed the city for thirty minutes, destroying 597 buildings, killing 213 and injuring almost 1,000 people.

Q. Who frequently included the following quote when he apologized to his guests for serving vegetarian meals: "The elephant is the strongest animal. He also cannot stand meat"?

A. Adolf Hitler.

Q. "Where have you come from?" Who asked it?

A. Major General Josef Reichert, Commanding Officer of the German 711th Division to two British paratroopers who landed on the lawn of his headquarters and were promptly captured. One of them, however, responded, "Awfully sorry, old man, but we simply landed here by accident."

Q. Who said, "It is assumed that there are no enemy [aircraft] carriers in waters adjacent to Midway"?

A. Japanese Admiral Chuichi Nagumo, on June 4, 1942, prior to the start of the Battle of Midway.

Q. Who wrote the following in Latin in the customs station in Belgium as he left: "Ungrateful Belgium, you will not possess my bones"?

A. General Ernst von Falkenhausen, German governor-general of Belgium, who had done his utmost to prevent the SS and Gestapo from their campaign of horror in that country. Falkenhausen was sentenced to twelve years in prison by the Belgians after the war but was released within a month as an act of clemency. One of the conspirators in the plot to kill Hitler, he had been imprisoned in Dachau also but escaped death when the U.S. liberated the death camp.

Q. Who popularized the phrase "unconditional surrender"?

A. FDR, at the Casablanca Conference, January 24, 1943. He is said to have believed that the term was an expansion of General Grant's initials (U.S.) after Grant's demand for unconditional surrender of Fort Donelson in February 1862.

Q. What did the following message mean: "The Italian Navigator has just landed in the New World. The natives are friendly"?

A. Sent by Nobel prize-winner physicist Arthur Compton, it informed Washington that the U.S. had successfully produced a controlled chain reaction with the atom.

Q. Who sent the following message: "Our casualties heavy. Enemy casualties unknown. Situation: we are winning"? About what?

A. U.S. Marine Corps Colonel David Shoup to the Navy ships off Betio during the initial engagements of the Tarawa campaign.

Q. What did the following mean: "The long sobs of the violins of autumn"?

A. It was the first half of the message on the BBC announcing the D-Day invasion to the French underground and, because they knew what it would be, to German counterintelligence.

Q. What was the second half of the D-Day message broadcast to the French underground troops re the Normandy landings?

A. "Wounds my heart with a monotonous languor." Both the first and second parts of the message are from a nineteenth-century poem by French poet Paul Verlaine, "Song of Autumn."

Q. Whose wartime diary contains the following, dated November 25, 1941: "The President predicted that we were likely to be attacked perhaps next Monday ... the question was how we should maneuver them into the position of firing the first shot"?

A. U.S. Secretary of War Henry L. Stimson's. It covered events discussed in a cabinet meeting over the possibility of hostilities with Japan.

Q. What was the legend above the portico on the Reichstag?

A. Dem Deutschen Volke (To the German people).

Q. What did the BBC code message "It is hot in Suez" indicate?

A. Sabotage by the French of railroad equipment and tracks. It was broadcast at 6:30 P.M. the night before D-Day.

Q. Which American unit posted the following sign and where was it: "Truman Bridge, Gateway to Berlin"?

A. At Barby, Germany, on the east bank of the Elbe. The rest of the sign read, "Courtesy of the 83rd Infantry Division." It went up less than twenty-four hours after Harry S. Truman took the reins of government in April 1945.

Q. Who asked, "Does anybody here know the road to Paris?"

A. Captain Raymond Drone of the 2nd French Armored Division on August 24, 1944, as he set out to become the first French officer to return to Paris with a small column of men and vehicles.

Q. Who sent the following message to Hitler on April 22, 1945: "My Fuehrer, in view of your decision to remain in the fortress of Berlin do you agree that I take over at once the total leadership of the Reich?"

A. Hermann Goering, who was promptly arrested by the SS for his grab at power.

Q. Who said, "A million men cannot take Tarawa in a hundred years"?

A. Japanese Admiral Keji Shibasaki. To his boast 5,600 Marines responded by taking Tarawa in seventy-two hours.

Q. Of whom did Churchill say, "A man of genius who might well have become also a man of destiny"?

A. British Major General Orde Wingate, who was killed in a plane crash on March 24, 1944. The other "man of destiny" the PM referred to was Charles de Gaulle.

Q. Who said, "Gee, I didn't know our bombers had done *that* much damage in Rome"?

A. An unidentified American GI who, upon entering the Eternal City, had his first glimpse of the ruins of the Colosseum.

Q. What did Hitler say after seeing tanks being tested at Kumersdorf?

A. "That's what I need. That's what I want to have." The date was February 1935.

Q. Who said, "If the Germans ever get here they will never go home"?

A. Mussolini, in 1940, discussing the "advantage" of having German troops on Italian soil.

FACT Six Japanese cities were destroyed by a single 855-plane B-29 raid on August 2, 1945, that dropped several tons of jellied gasoline and magnesium bombs. This was four days before the first atom bomb was dropped.

U.S. Army Photo

Q. When did U.S. President Franklin D. Roosevelt first publicly announce the Four Freedoms?

A. During his State of the Union address to Congress in January 1941. He had been elected to an unprecedented third term the previous November and would go on to yet a fourth term. The Four Freedoms are freedom of speech, freedom of worship, freedom from fear, and freedom from want.

Q. Who said, "Never have so few been commanded by so many"?

A. Major General Maxwell Taylor, who with his staff of the 101st Airborne landed amid a small group of enlisted paratroopers during the Normandy airborne drop.

Q. Who said, "If bombs drop on Germany, my name is Meyer"?

A. Head of the German Luftwaffe, Hermann Goering, in 1939. The Reichsmarschall regretted the remark on August 24, 1940, when the RAF succeeded in bombing Berlin for the first time.

Q. What battle did this Churchill quote describe: "I had hoped that we were hurling a wildcat onto the shore, but all we got was a stranded whale"?

A. The Allied landings at Anzio and Nettuno, Italy.

Q. Who said, "Hoist the colors and let no enemy ever haul them down"?

A. MacArthur upon returning to Corregidor.

Q. "Two eyes for an eye." Whose battle cry was this?

A. The Red Army's as it pushed toward Berlin.

Q. Who said, "I do not understand the words, but by God I like your spirit"?

A. Stalin to Churchill during a meeting in Moscow between the two heads of state. The Soviet leader had insulted the ability of the British to fight. Churchill burst into a torrent of oratory that was so forceful and fast the interpreters were unable to keep up.

Q. Who radioed the memorable message of the sinking of the Japanese aircraft carrier *Shoho*—"Scratch one flattop"?

A. Navy pilot Lieutenant Commander Robert Dixon during the Battle of the Coral Sea, May 4–8, 1942. The *Shoho* marked the first time the U.S. had sunk a Japanese ship larger than a destroyer.

Q. Who said, "Saw steamer, strafed same, sank same, some sight, signed Smith"?

A. Captain Fred M. Smith, U.S. Army Air Force, flying a P-38 during the campaign in the Aleutians. Smith sent the witty message after an encounter with a Japanese destroyer.

Q. Who said, "If Hitler were to invade hell, I should find occasion to make a favorable reference to the devil"?

A. Winston Churchill, after being questioned about his kindly remarks about Russia (he was widely known as an anti-communist) and Britain's support of her after the German invasion.

Q. Who said, "It is more likely that the United States ... will be attacked by the not-well-known but very warlike inhabitants of the planet Mars"?

A. Mussolini, in an address to the Italian people on February 23, 1941, in which he denied that the Axis powers had any plans to attack the U.S.

Q. Who said, The "British, the Jewish, and the Roosevelt administration [are] the three most important groups ... pressing this country toward war"?

A. American aviation hero Charles Lindbergh during an address in Des Moines, Iowa, on September 12, 1941. This is the worst side of Lindbergh; he performed valuable and unheralded service later as a flier in combat situations.

Q. Who said, "This is not the end. It is not even the beginning of the end. But it is, perhaps, the end of the beginning"?

A. Prime Minister Winston Churchill in remarks about the British victory in Egypt on November 10, 1942.

Q. Where does the following inscription appear?

> We Polish soldiers
> For our freedom and yours
> Have given our souls to God
> Our bodies to the soil of Italy
> And our hearts to Poland.

A. At the Polish cemetery established after the battle for Monte Cassino, where 1,200 Poles died.

Q. Who said, "I give the gift of myself to France. ... The fighting must stop"?

A. Marshal Henri Pétain, upon becoming Premier on May 17, 1940, as German troops were overwhelming the French.

Q. What was the last message Hitler sent via teletype out of the bunker in Berlin before he committed suicide?

A. "Where is Wenck? Where is Steiner?" He was referring to the two generals on whom the final defense of the city had fallen. The message was transmitted by Gerda Niedieck, a teletype operator.

Q. Where did the message "Good luck to you all" come from before the Berlin telegraph office closed down on April 22, 1945?

A. Tokyo. It was the last message received.

Q. Who said, "I am insulted by the persistent assertion that I want war. Am I a fool? War! It would settle nothing"?

A. Adolf Hitler during an interview on November 10, 1933.

Q. Which well-known American broadcast newsman made the following quip after Italy joined the war: "Italy looks like a boot and behaves like a heel"?

A. Walter Winchell.

Q. Who made the following predictions about World War II: "Japan will attack the Hawaiian Islands and damage the American fleet-... they will employ a pincers movement against the Philippines"?

A. Similar in content to predictions by Billy Mitchell, which would come years later, the above comments were published in *The Valor of Ignorance* by American author Homer Lea in 1909.

FACT The United States resettlement of Americans of Japanese ancestry which began after the December 7, 1941, attack on Pearl Harbor was still being investigated by the U.S. government forty years later. Hearings in Washington, D.C., by the Commission on Wartime Relocation and Internment of Civilians heard charges that the ten resettlement camps "behind barbed wire fences" were incarceration centers. The defense of the action included testimony by former Assistant Secretary of War John McCloy who said: "There has been, in my judgment, at times a spate of quite irresponsible comment to the effect that this wartime move was callous, shameful and induced by racial or punitive motives. It was nothing of the sort." One CWRIC member, William Marutani, an American of Japanese ancestry who became a judge in Pennsylvania, challenged McCloy's comments with the question: "What other Americans fought for this country while their parents, brothers and sisters were incarcerated?"

Quotes on War in General

"In time of war the first casualty is truth."
—Boake Carter

"In wartime, truth is so precious that she should always be attended by a bodyguard of lies."
—Winston Churchill

"Never think that war, no matter how necessary, nor how justified, is not a crime."
—Ernest Hemingway

"Better pointed bullets than pointed speeches."
—Otto von Bismarck

"War can only be abolished through war."
—Mao Tse-tung

"There are no warlike peoples, just warlike leaders."
—Ralph Bunche

"The way to win an atomic war is to make certain it never starts."
—Omar Bradley

"Diplomacy has rarely been able to gain at the conference table what cannot be gained or held on the battlefield."
—Walter Bedell Smith

"War is too important to be left to the generals."
—*Georges Clemenceau*

"In war, when a commander becomes so bereft of reason and perspective that he fails to understand the dependence of arms on divine guidance, he no longer deserves victory."
—*Douglas MacArthur*

"War hath no fury like a non-combatant."
—*C. E. Montague*

"You furnish the pictures, I'll furnish the war."
—*William Randolph Hearst*

"War would end if the dead could return."
—*Stanley Baldwin*

"Do not needlessly endanger your lives until I give you the signal."
—*Dwight D. Eisenhower*

"When women have a voice in national and international affairs, war will cease forever."
—*Augusta Stowe-Gullen*

"The day when nobody comes back from a war it will be because the war has at last been properly organized."
—*Boris Vian*

FACT The legendary Allied convoy lines to Murmansk and Archangel, Russia, were actually safer than similar convoy runs to Britain. The percentage of ships lost in the Arctic was 7.2 vs. 22.6 bound for Britain. However, one of the ships lost in the Arctic, the HMS *Edinburgh,* went down with 372 Russian gold bars which was payment for war materiel. In late summer 1981 a salvage team had recovered one hundred of the bars, valued at more than $20 million, and expected to bring up the rest. The U.S. government had no claim for the treasure as it had settled its claim and been compensated years earlier.

The War on Land

Q. Name the three American beaches at Normandy on D-Day?

A. There were only *two:* Utah and Omaha. The British had three: Gold, Juno and Sword.

Q. Who was the American baseball player who performed espionage for the U.S. while on a visit to Japan as a member of a U.S. baseball team in 1934?

A. Morris (Mo) Berg, who was joined on the trip by Babe Ruth and Lou Gehrig. Berg took photographs of restricted areas that were later used by U.S. pilots on bombing missions. He was the only player on the trip with a letter of introduction to the U.S. diplomatic and consular officers from Secretary of State Cordell Hull.

Q. Where was the first battle contact by Allied airborne troops in France on D-Day?

A. At the Caen Canal and Orne River bridges, by the British 6th Airborne. It lasted about fifteen minutes and ended in favor of the Allies.

Q. Name the famous British actor who died when the Germans shot down a commercial airliner they thought Winston Churchill was aboard.

A. Leslie Howard, who was nominated twice for Academy Awards. He also played Ashley Wilkes in *Gone With the Wind.*

U.S. Army Photo

FACT: The Ludendorff railroad bridge at Remagen, Germany, the only Rhine crossing that had not been destroyed, collapsed ten days after the first Allied troops began to cross it in March 1945. Four hours after this photo was taken, on March 17, the bridge crumbled. Some 400 troops of the U.S. First Army were on it at the time.

U.S. Coast Guard Photo

Q. How many Allied troops participated in the Normandy invasion?

A. There were nearly 3 million combat and support personnel from the Allied powers involved in the operation. About 1.7 million were from the U.S.

Q. Identify the SS officer who commanded the German incident on the radio station at Gleiwitz which Germany used as an excuse for invading Poland.

A. Alfred Naujocks, who personally received the orders from Reinhard Heydrich less than a month before the incident on September 1, 1939.

Q. What was the first battle in the Pacific where the Japanese defended territory the Empire held prior to its conquests in the war?

A. Kwajalein, the largest atoll in the world, measuring eighteen miles wide by 78 miles long.

Q. Who was the head of the branch of the Signal Corps responsible for producing U.S. propaganda films?

A. Colonel Frank Capra, who was aided by Lieutenant Colonel Darryl F. Zanuck, Major John Huston, and Lieutenant Colonel Anatole Litvak, among others. In all, 132 members of the Screen Directors Guild were among the 40,000 Hollywood people in uniform.

Q. Who was the French general who escaped from a German prison camp in France and was smuggled to Gibraltar by the Allies?

A. General Henri Honoré Giraud, who became the military chief of North Africa and was a serious threat to de Gaulle as the Frenchman who would lead all Free French forces. Captured in May 1940, he escaped from occupied France in April 1942.

Q. Name the Russian general who "captured" Berlin?

A. Colonel General Vasili I. Chuikov, commander of the Eighth Guards Army, who once advised Chiang Kai-shek.

Q. Who succeeded Mussolini as Italian Premier?

A. General Pietro Badoglio, an anti-Facist, in July 1943. He surrendered to the Allies in September and declared war on Germany in October.

FACT The U.S. Navy fleet which was to come under attack at Pearl Harbor left the U.S. West Coast for maneuvers around Hawaii on April 2, 1940. On May 7, President Roosevelt ordered it to remain indefinitely in Hawaii.

Q. Who offered to recognize the Soviet claims in the Dardanelles and permit the U.S.S.R. freedom in the Balkans in return for a "common policy of self-protection" against Germany?

A. Winston Churchill, through Britain's ambassador to Moscow. This was in 1940, when Germany and the Soviet Union were still on "good terms." The proposal was never renewed.

Q. Name the German commando who rescued Mussolini on September 12, 1943.

A. Otto Skorzeny, who had been asked by Hitler himself to bring the Italian dictator back to Berlin. Shorzeny's ninety men landed by glider in the Abruzzi Mountains and overwhelmed the garrison of 250 men guarding Mussolini.

Q. What was the pact that Germany, Italy and Japan signed on September 27, 1940?

A. The Tripartite Pact. It obliged the signatories to come to each other's aid in the event the U.S. joined the war.

Q. Who was the American Vice President when the U.S. entered the war in December, 1941?

A. Henry A. Wallace, who was elected with FDR in the 1940 election.

Q. Which of the three British beaches at Normandy was the costliest?

A. Juno, which was the task of the Canadian troops.

Q. Identify the medical equipment that was taken everywhere Hitler went.

A. A complete set of dental tools and supplies. He had taken poor care of his teeth in his younger days.

Q. Name the first German city captured by U.S. troops.

A. Aachen, which is famous in history as the fortress of Charlemagne.

FACT   American aviation hero Charles Lindbergh resigned his commission as a U.S. Army Air Corps reserve colonel on April 28, 1941, after President Roosevelt criticized a speech Lindbergh had made. FDR called the Lone Eagle an appeaser and a defeatist. After Pearl Harbor, however, he served with distinction.

Q. Identify the only amphibious invasion thrown back with a loss.

A. The Japanese attempt to take Wake Island on December 11, 1942. A few days later they tried again and succeeded.

Q. Which battle was America's worst defeat in the war?

A. The Ardennes Forest, just before Christmas 1944, when approximately 12,000 out of 16,000 troops of the 106th U.S. Infantry Divisions were killed, wounded or captured by the Germans.

Q. Identify the Frenchman who ran the Resistance for de Gaulle until he was captured and killed in June 1943.

A. Jean Moulin, known as Max. Captured initially in 1940 by the Nazis, he slit his own throat and thereafter wore a scarf to conceal the ugly scar. His second capture in 1943 was by the Gestapo.

Q. Identify the highest-ranking traitor in the war.

A. General Andrei Andreyevitch Vlasov, a hero during the attack on Moscow, was captured by the Germans and cast his lot with them. He built up an army of Soviet prisoners who fought for Germany until May 1945. Captured by Patton and turned over to the Russians, he was hanged.

Q. Identify the Norwegian whose name became a synonym for traitor.

A. Vidkun Quisling, who, after the Germans captured Norway in April 1940, proclaimed himself Prime Minister in their behalf. The Nazis rejected him within the week but did return him to that post in 1942. He was executed as a traitor by the Norwegians after the war.

Q. Identify the Italian commander who invaded Egypt from Libya in September 1940.

A. Marshal Rodolfo Graziani, who was pushed 500 miles back into Libya by Wavell's Army of the Nile.

FACT   Despite the fame the German panzer divisions earned with blitz tactics, only four divisions were totally mechanized. The other eighty-six German divisions at the outbreak of war depended largely on horses for mobility. By war's end slightly more than 2.7 million horses had been used by the German war machine on all fronts.

Ullstein Photo

FACT: Through the efforts of Germany's armaments minister, Albert Speer, left, the German Army was better equipped as late as 1944 than it had been when the Nazis invaded Russia in 1941. With Speer in this May 1945 photo after the German surrender are Admiral Karl Doenitz, Hitler's successor, and General Alfred Jodl, chief of operations at OKW and Hitler's personal chief of staff. Speer and Doenitz were sentenced to prison terms at the Nuremberg trials. Jodl was hanged.

Q. Identify the German general, second in command to Rommel, who was captured in November 1942 when Montgomery drove the Germans out of Egypt.

A. General Ritter von Thoma was captured along with 30,000 Axis troops.

Q. Which countries produced the heaviest, which the lightest tanks?

A. Germany's 74.8-ton Tiger II tanks, which measured 33′9″, were the largest. Italy's L-3 at 3.4 tons and 10′5″ in length was the smallest. The largest/heaviest tank in the U.S. arsenal was the 41.1-ton, 28′10″-long Pershing. Germany had another 74.8-ton tank, the Elephant, but it was a tiny 22′3″ in length compared to the Tiger II.

Q. Who was the first British general to land in Normandy?

A. Major General Richard Gale, commander of the 6th Airborne.

Q. Who designed the SS uniforms and insignia?

A. Carl Diebitsch, who was later the artistic director of the first profit-making business run by the SS, the porcelain factory at Dachau.

Q. Of the 4,500 Japanese troops on Betio Island in the Tarawa Atoll how many lived to be taken prisoner?

A. Seventeen. The rest followed orders to fight to the last man.

Q. To what concentration camp did General Patton order the residents of a nearby village be brought to view the conditions they claimed to know nothing about?

A. Ohrdruf, on April 13, 1945. The next day the mayor and his wife hanged themselves.

Q. Identify the French general who conquered Monte Cassino in Italy.

A. Alphonse Juin.

Q. Who was the commissar of Kharkov, the city known as the Soviet Pittsburgh?

A. Nikita Khrushchev, who called the Kremlin and demanded that the Soviet Army be withdrawn in the face of German strength.

Q. Identify the Axis general responsible for defending Sicily.

A. General Alfredo Guzzoni, commanding general of the Italian Sixth Army.

U.S. Army Signal Corps Photo

Q. Identify the two highest-ranking Axis officers captured in North Africa.

A. German General Jurgen von Arnim, seen here the day after his capture on Cape Bon Peninsula following the surrender of Tunis and Bizerte, and Italian Field Marshal Alessandro Messe. Behind Von Armin in photo is German General Kramer.

Q. What was the name of the site near Kiev where the SS murdered almost 34,000 Jews by gunfire?

A. Babi Yar ravine. The Jews were told to assemble for resettlement. The Germans, who expected no more than 6,000 to appear, were surprised that so many actually turned up.

Q. What were the four things that Eisenhower said won the war for the Allies?

A. The bazooka, the jeep, the A-bomb and the DC-3.

Q. Why was the city of Lidice leveled?

A. On May 29, 1942, two Czech freedom fighters tossed a bomb into the car of Reinhard Heydrich, chief of the security police, and the SD "Hangman" Heydrich died on June 4. In revenge the Nazis killed 1,331 Czechs and selected the village of Lidice to be burned down, the ruins dynamited and leveled off.

Q. Which British ground commander held the distinction of never having lost a battle?

A. The man whom Eisenhower considered an inadequate strategist, Bernard Law Montgomery.

Q. Who was Colonel Count Klaus Schenk von Stauffenberg?

A. The German officer who placed the bomb in Hitler's headquarters at Rastenburg. The original plan was to kill Hitler, Goering and Himmler at Berchtesgaden, but it was postponed twice because Hitler was alone both times. Finally, on July 20, 1944, the plan was carried out, but failed. While four Germans were killed in the explosion, Hitler survived, the plot was aborted and the plotters were eventually caught and executed.

Q. Who was Stauffenberg's chief co-conspirator in the plot to kill Hitler on July 20, 1944?

A. General Friedrich Olbricht, deputy commander of the Home Army in Germany.

Q. Who was the Japanese commander on Iwo Jima?

A. Lieutenant General Tadamichi Kuribayashi, who commanded over 20,000 troops to defend the eight-square-mile island when the U.S. Marines invaded in 1945.

U.S. Army Photo

Q. Which Allied general at one time advocated celibacy for those serious about pursuing a military career?

A. When Bernard Law Montgomery was a young officer he held that belief. Here Montgomery chats with his boss, Dwight D. Eisenhower, in Holland on November 29, 1944.

Q. Of the approximately 75,000 men on the Bataan Death March, how many were Americans?

A. Twelve thousand. Most of the rest were Filipinos.

Q. How many Allied prisoners of war actually marched, or walked, on the Death March?

A. About half of those involved rode in trucks and suffered little. However, the atrocities to many who did walk were enough to justify the name Death March. Seven to ten thousand died.

Q. Which branch of the German armed forces was known as the Nazi Service because of the high number of party members in it?

A. The Luftwaffe, which was under the command of Reichsmarschall Hermann Goering.

Q. Identify the village in France where the 101st Airborne first exchanged fire with the enemy?

A. According to division records it was at Foucarville, behind Utah Beach, where eleven troopers attacked machine gun, anti-tank gun and dugout positions.

Q. What was the name of General Eisenhower's British chauffeur?

A. Kay Summersby.

Q. What song did the British troops in the Africa campaign "steal" from the Afrika Korps and take as their own?

A. "Lili Marlene."

Q. What was the name of the site where German scientists worked on rocket research?

A. Peenemunde, in Poland.

FACT For the low-level bombing that Lieutenant Colonel Jimmy Doolittle's B-25s had to perform in their attack on Japan in 1942 it was discovered that the regular bombsights were ineffective. Captain C. R. Greening, a pilot in the 17th Bombardment Group, which flew the mission, created a device for a cost of approximately fifteen cents per bombsight which worked perfectly.

U.S. Army Photo

Q. What kind of children's toy did American paratroopers use to exchange identification signals after the D-Day drops into Fortress Europe?

A. Tin snapper cricket toys. A single snap required two in answer. The 82nd Airborne, however, added a password just to be sure. This group happily displays a Nazi flag captured near St. Marcouf, France.

U.S. Army Photo

Q. Name the two French ports that remained in German hands until they surrendered at the end of the war.

A. Lorient and St. Nazaire. In contrast, Carentan was the first French town liberated by the Allies on June 12, 1944. This photo shows U.S. troops moving through Carentan streets and away from St. Lô and Paris (note sign on wall above GI at far right).

Q. Who led the Japanese suicide charge on Attu Island against U.S. 7th Division troops?

A. Colonel Yasuyo Yamasaki, on May 29, 1943, screaming "Japanese drink blood like wine."

Q. Identify the first U.S. forces from the Normandy beaches to link up with U.S. airborne forces dropped before the beach invasions began.

A. Troopers from the 101st Airborne and soldiers from the 4th Division, behind Utah Beach.

Q. On what grounds did the Germans justify the right to use Soviet POW's to work in essential war production?

A. By noting that the Soviets were not signers of the Geneva Convention, and therefore should not come under its protection.

Q. What was the name of Mussolini's mistress?

A. Clara Petacci. She, along with the Duce, was shot by Italian partisans near Lake Como on April 28, 1945.

Q. Who signed Clark Gable's discharge papers in June 1944?

A. Fellow actor, and future President of the United States, Captain Ronald Reagan.

Q. Where did Hitler do his famous "jig," which was actually the work of clever Allied film editing?

A. Though it was reported to have been done at Compiègne, site of the French surrender, Hitler was recorded on film at his headquarters at Bruly-de-Pesche, Belgium, after having received word that Marshal Pétain was asking for an armistice.

FACT On September 11, 1944, U.S. submarines sank two Japanese transport ships that had over 2,218 U.S., British and Australian prisoners of war. These troops were survivors of the building of the bridge on the River Kwai. Nearly 1,300 of the POWs were killed when the *Rakuyo Maru* and the *Kachidoki Maru* sank within minutes. The U.S. submarines rescued 159, and Japanese ships picked up another 792 and reimprisoned them. Only 606 of the original 2,218 survived the war.

National Archives Photo

FACT: Japan's ambassador in Washington, Admiral Kichisaburo Nomura, advised Tokyo that the U.S. was reading the Japanese diplomatic code on May 20, 1941, more than six months before the hostilities between the two countries began. Tokyo responded by telling its Washington embassy to have all sensitive messages handled by only one person. As a result, on December 7, 1941, Nomura (right) checks the time as he and special envoy Saburo Kurusu wait in the U.S. State Department to see Secretary Cordell Hull. Only a relatively short time before they arrived did the two Japanese diplomats themselves receive the slowly decoded message that war was to begin this day.

27679

Q. Who was the only general to land with the first wave of troops on Normandy?

A. Brigadier General Theodore Roosevelt, 4th Division, on Utah Beach.

Q. Which German units got closest to Moscow, and how close did they get?

A. The 3rd and 4th Panzer Groups got to within twenty-five miles of the Russian capital in December 1941.

Q. Identify the Norwegian king who, with his ministers, set up a government in exile in Britain.

A. King Haakon VII.

Q. Identify the European monarch who died under questionable circumstances after a visit with Adolf Hitler.

A. King Boris III of Bulgaria, who had never been one of the Axis powers' great supporters, died on August 28, 1943. Though his death was listed as by natural causes, it is believed he was assassinated.

Q. Who stopped Rommel in North Africa?

A. British General Sir Claude Auchinleck at El Alamein. Churchill replaced him with Generals Alexander and Montgomery, who followed with several successes.

Q. Identify the SS division responsible for protecting Hitler at his Rastenburg headquarters.

A. The Gross Deutschland Division.

Q. What did the initials SHAEF stand for?

A. Supreme Headquarters Allied Expeditionary Force. General Dwight D. Eisenhower, U.S. Army, commanded.

FACT Heinrich Himmler ordered the creation of an extermination camp at Auschwitz, Poland, on April 27, 1940. Of the 3.3-million Jews in Poland less than 10 percent would be alive by the time the exterminations at Auschwitz ended on October 30, 1944. In addition, the camp was responsible for the deaths of Jews transported there from other occupied areas.

Q. Where was the heaviest concentration of German troops on D-Day?

A. At La Roche-Guyon, the headquarters of Field Marshal Erwin Rommel's Army Group B, the most powerful German military presence in France. There were more than three German soldiers per villager.

Q. Who were the first victims of poison gas extermination at Auschwitz?

A. Russian prisoners of war on September 3, 1941.

Q. Where was the only place in Paris where the Tricolor was visible during the German Occupation?

A. At Les Invalides, the Army Museum.

Q. Where and when did the French Tricolor fly for the first time after the German occupation of Paris in 1940?

A. At the Prefecture of Police on the Ile de la Cité across from Notre Dame, August 19, 1944. It had not been flown from a public building in over four years and two months. Paris would be liberated six days later.

Q. Where did Soviet troops raise their country's flag in Berlin?

A. Atop the Reichstag building, on April 13, 1945, while the battle of Berlin was still going on.

Q. When did German troops occupy Athens?

A. April 27, 1941. The Nazi flag was hung from the Parthenon before 9 A.M.

Q. Who was the first member of the U.S. Congress to enlist after Pearl Harbor?

A. Representative Lyndon Baines Johnson of Texas, later senator, senate majority leader and President of the United States.

Q. Who was the only member of the U.S. Congress to vote no after FDR said that "a state of war existed" between the U.S. and Japan?

A. Representative Jeanette Rankin (R., Mont.). She had also voted no against the resolution for war with Germany in 1917.

U.S. Army Photo

Q. Name the German town where the Western Allies and the Russians linked up in April 1945.

A. At 4:40 P.M. on April 25 in Torgau on the Elbe, Lieutenant William D. Robertson of Los Angeles, U.S. 69th Division, First Army, met soldiers of Marshal Koniev's First Ukrainian Army on the twisted and sloping girders of a blown-out bridge spanning the Elbe. In photo, Robertson and Soviet Lieutenant Sylvashko re-enact their first embrace. However, Lieutenant Albert Kotzebue, also of the U.S. 69th, and a patrol of troops crossed the Elbe at 1:30 P.M. and reported meeting Russian soldiers in Strehla. This would have been three hours before Robertson's Torgau meeting, which is considered the official meeting.

USIS Photo

FACT: Charles de Gaulle was nearly shot by a German Navy officer, Lieutenant Commander Harry Leithold, as Leithold watched the French general's return to Paris from the Kriegsmarine headquarters on the Place de la Concorde. However, after capturing de Gaulle in the sights of his submachine gun, Leithold realized that the crowd around the man outside would easily seize and kill him. Leithold decided that the tall Frenchman in the vehicle wasn't worth it, no matter who he was. Later in a POW camp Leithold saw a newspaper photo of de Gaulle and realized who it was he had almost shot. Other snipers, even after the German surrender, continued to break up crowds at the world-famous square. Parisians in photo above scatter as shots rang out on August 26, 1944.

Q. Name the first geographic area to be awarded a medal during the war.

A. The island of Malta, which received the George Cross from Britain for its heroic stand against the Axis.

Q. What was the worst military disaster ever suffered by a European nation in the Orient?

A. The fall of Singapore on February 15, 1942, along with the surrender of more than 70,000 troops and civilians.

Q. Identify the Polish general who led troops that had been liberated from POW camps in Russia and fought in the Middle East.

A. General Wladyslaw Anders, whose troops also had the distinction of capturing the abbey at Monte Cassino.

Q. Identify the only two civilian activities in Berlin that did not cease during the attack, surrender and occupation of the city.

A. The seventeen breweries and the weather bureau operated without interruption.

Q. Identify the Japanese general who did what was thought impossible and crossed the Owen Stanley Mountains in New Guinea.

A. General Horii, who drowned in a river crossing when the Australians and Americans counterattacked in September–October 1942. The Japanese had come to within thirty miles of Port Moresby.

Q. Identify the first American unit to cross the Rhine.

A. A unit of the 9th Armored Division, First Army, crossed the Ludendorff bridge at Remagen on March 7, 1945.

FACT   At the outbreak of war in Europe, Dwight D. Eisenhower was a lieutenant colonel on the staff of General Douglas MacArthur in the Philippines. By the time the Japanese attacked Pearl Harbor, Eisenhower had accepted command of a tank regiment in a division headed by General George S. Patton. Prior to his first assignment to London during the war, Ike had only been to Europe once previously, to write a guidebook on American war monuments. He rose from lieutenant colonel to general in less than eighteen months.

Q. Identify the Egyptian military officer who located a mansion on the Rue des Pyramides that was to be used by Erwin Rommel once the field marshal arrived in Cairo.

A. Anwar el-Sadat, who, along with Gamal Abdel Nasser, was part of the anti-British Free Officers Movement in the army.

Q. Identify the two generals, one from the allies, the other from the Axis, who had a fondness for parakeets.

A. Montgomery of the British and Blumentritt of the Wehrmacht. Both men kept several of the birds with them whenever possible.

Q. Name the site where the British first defeated the Japanese in a land battle.

A. At Sinzweya, Burma, on February 23, 1944.

Q. Who was the youngest general in the German Army?

A. General Walther Wenck, forty-five, former chief of staff to Guderian and the man all Berliners depended on to save the city from the Russians.

Q. What was the first U.S. offensive in the Pacific against Japanese ground troops that resulted in a U.S. victory?

A. Guadalcanal, which was also Japan's first land defeat.

Q. Who was the Allied general the Germans respected above all others?

A. General George Smith Patton. They simply couldn't believe the allies would not use him to lead the D-Day invasion, and they waited for "Army Group Patton" to storm the Pas de Calais instead of Normandy.

FACT The largest aircraft carrier of any navy became part of the Japanese fleet on November 11, 1944, when the *Shinano* (with a thirty-centimeter-thick deck over concrete) went on-line. However, this ship recorded the briefest period of sea duty of any major ship in the war. The U.S. submarine *Archerfish* torpedoed her and she sank on November 29 in the Kumano Sea. The sinking of the 59,000-ton leviathan was the largest submarine kill of the war.

U.S. Army Photo

FACT: Hitler created an award for German mothers, the Mother's Cross, that was awarded in bronze, silver and gold, depending on the number of children they bore for the Reich. The *Mutterkreuz* was an amalgam of the Iron Cross, the Nazi Party Badge and the Pour le Mérite. To earn the gold version the German mother had to have eight or more children. Initiated in 1938, it was intended to honor women much in the same way soldiers earned citations for exceptional service. The *Mutterkreuz* awards were given out each year on the anniversary of Hitler's own mother's birth, August 12.

U.S. Army Photo

FACT: Not all French citizens hated the Germans or gave wholehearted support to the underground Resistance movement. In photo above two women are paraded through the Paris streets with their heads shaved, barefooted and with swastikas painted on their heads. This was the price they paid for collaborating with the enemy. This scene was recorded on August 27, 1944.

U.S. Army Photo

FACT: U.S. General Courtney Hicks Hodges was forced to leave the U.S. Military Academy at West Point in 1906 because he failed geometry. He immediately enlisted as a private in the Army and was commissioned as a second lieutenant in 1909, only one year behind his former classmates. During World War II the U.S. First Army, while under his command, liberated Paris, defeated the Germans in the Ardennes, made the first Rhine crossing at Remagen and met the Russians on the Elbe.

Q. Which Allied army had the greatest representation of foreign units in it?

A. The British Second Army, under Sir Miles Dempsey, included Irish, Scottish, Polish, Czech, Belgian, Dutch, U.S. and British units.

Q. What area did Churchill frequently refer to as "the soft underbelly" of Europe?

A. The Balkans.

Q. Identify the first German officer to sight the Normandy invasion fleet.

A. Major Werner Pluskat, who commanded four batteries of the German 352nd Division with its twenty guns over Omaha Beach. When he called division headquarters and was asked where the ships were heading he replied, "Right for me."

Q. Who were the three army group commanders directly under Eisenhower in Europe?

A. Generals Bradley, Montgomery and Devers.

Q. Identify the U.S. General who was smuggled into Italy to negotiate the surrender of the Italians.

A. General Maxwell D. Taylor, artillery chief of the 82nd Airborne, who went via a British PT boat, Italian corvette and land vehicles into occupied Rome to meet with General Carboni. This was prior to the invasion of Italy.

Q. Which Allied commander boasted that his army had liberated more square miles of Europe, traveled farther than any other and caused more German casualties?

A. Patton.

FACT   The Russians turned on more than 140 large antiaircraft lights at 4 A.M. on Monday, April 16, 1945, as they began their bombardment across the Oder which started the battle for Berlin. The lights were intended to confuse defending German troops but actually provided German artillery with a better view of the advancing Russians.

U.S. Army Photo

Q. Identify the U.S. Army unit that broke the deadlock after the Normandy invasion and crossed the St. Lô-Périers road.

A. The VII Corps of the First Army under General J. Lawton "Lightning Joe" Collins. Within two days after their success on July 25, 1944, they were well on their way down the Cotentin Peninsula. Collins, like his boss, Omar Bradley, was known as a GI's general.

Q. What became of Karol Wojtyla, the Polish student who remained on Gestapo execution lists for years because of helping Jews escape?

A. Ordained a priest in 1946, he became Pope John Paul II in 1978.

Q. Identify the only U.S. Army division to employ a captured German plane and use it for scouting.

A. The 83rd Infantry Division. The plane was a Messerschmitt 109, which they painted olive green.

Q. Where did the first Axis assault on a U.S. mainland military base take place?

A. At Fort Stevens, Oregon, on June 22, 1942, when a Japanese submarine fired at the coastal outpost. The last time a U.S. mainland military outpost had been fired on was during the War of 1812. There were no casualties in the Fort Stevens incident.

Q. Identify the first U.S. mainland civilian location to come under enemy fire in the war.

A. The oil fields west of Santa Barbara, California, which were fired on by Japanese submarine I-17 on February 23, 1942.

Q. What was the common name for the British explosive called Explosive C?

A. Plastic.

Q. What company, famous for expensive fast cars, designed the Tiger tanks for Germany?

A. Porsche.

FACT The debate about the U.S. decision to drop the atom bomb on Hiroshima and Nagasaki frequently calls attention to the fact that more destruction was caused by a B-29 raid on Tokyo, March 9–10, 1945, than the later atomic raids. More than 83,000 people died in the Tokyo raid, which employed incendiary bombs, as against 70,000 deaths in Hiroshima and 20,000 in Nagasaki. However, the Tokyo raid employed more than 275 B-29s, while only one bomb-dropping plane was used in each of the atom bomb raids.

U.S. Army Photo

Q. Where and when did units of Patton's Third Army first cross the Rhine?

A. At Oppenheim, near Mainz, on Thursday, March 22, 1945. Shown here are the members of the first tank crew of the 41st Tank Battalion, 11th Armored Division, Third U.S. Army, on the day of the crossing. The five men are: Corporal William Hasse, Palisades Park, N.J.; Private Marvin Aldridge, Burlington, N.C.; T/4 John Latimi, Bronx, N.Y.; Corporal Vincent Morreale, Trenton, N.J.; and Corporal Sidney Meyer, Bronx, N.Y. Name of the tank? *Flat Foot Floosie.*

Q. Because of the relatively large number of Japanese troops who surrendered, which battle is considered a turning point in the psychological aspect of the war in the Pacific?

A. Saipan. Although most of the Japanese 27,000-man force on that island fought to the death, several hundred were captured, a previously unheard of situation.

Q. Identify the husband and wife team credited with breaking the Japanese Purple Code.

A. Lieutenant Colonel William Friedman, chief of the U.S. Army Cryptanalysis Bureau in World War II, and his wife, Elizabeth, who was a cryptanalyst with the U.S. Navy. She also broke the Japanese Doll Woman Case code, which dealt with the locations of Allied warships.

Q. Who was the Vichy French Prime Minister when Germany occupied France totally in 1942?

A. Pierre Laval, who supported the move.

Q. Where was Rommel on June 6, 1944, during D-Day?

A. He had returned home to be with his wife on her birthday.

Q. Name the most decorated soldier in World War II.

A. By the time he was twenty years old Audie Murphy had become the most decorated U.S. soldier *ever*. He received the Congressional Medal of Honor and twenty seven other decorations.

Q. Who were: "Soldiers in sailor uniforms, with Marine training, doing civilian work at WPA wages"?

A. The thousands of plumbers, carpenters, electricians, power equipment operators and other civilian craftsmen who became Navy 'engineers' in the Construction Batallions. They were called Seabees (CBs) and were involved in every operation in the Pacific during the war.

Q. Identify the Japanese general who defended Saipan against the U.S. Marines.

A. General Yoshitsugu Saito commanded 32,000 troops there when the assault began on June 15, 1944.

Q. What was the German National Redoubt?

A. During the final weeks of the war in Europe, rumors that the Germans were gathering for a last-stand battle or holdout in the mountainous southern part of Germany persisted. They proved to be groundless but had greatly influenced Allied thinking.

Q. When did the Allies invade the French Riviera?

A. On August 15, 1944, French and American troops under General Alexander Patch landed on the southern coast of France at St. Tropez.

Q. What was the delightful surprise the U.S. Marines found on Guam when it was reoccupied?

A. Guam had been the Japanese main liquor distribution center for the Central Pacific. Scotch, beer, bourbon, rye and sake were left for the leathernecks in great amounts.

Q. Name the Russian general who committed suicide rather than surrender to the Germans near Vyazma in April 1942.

A. General Mikhail G. Yefremov of the Thirty-Third Army.

Q. What was the name of the Spanish legion that Franco sent to help the Germans against the Russians at Leningrad?

A. The Blue Legion, made up of about 14,000 Spanish troops. They arrived at the front in September 1941.

Q. From which country did the Allied troops involved in the raid on Dieppe come?

A. Canada. There were 3,369 casualties out of just over 5,000 troops.

Q. Which member of Hitler's inner circle was born in Alexandria, Egypt?

A. Rudolf Hess.

Q. What was the name of the Italian secret service?

A. Servizio Informazione Segreto, known commonly as SIM.

Q. What was the name of the Japanese secret police in Tokyo, often compared to the German Gestapo?

A. Kempeitai.

Q. Identify the only American labor union to violate the AFL and CIO pledge of not striking during the war.

A. The United Mine Workers, who, under John L. Lewis, walked off their jobs four times.

Q. What were the American casualties as a result of the Japanese attack on Pearl Harbor and other areas of Oahu?

A. A total of 2,403, including sixty-eight civilians.

Q. Who helped the Germans violate the Treaty of Versailles and build an army in excess of 100,000 men?

A. In a secret agreement, the Soviet Union allowed Germans to train in Russia while the Germans trained Soviet officers and built arms plants for the U.S.S.R.

Q. Who was responsible for German espionage before and during the war?

A. Admiral Wilhelm Canaris, chief of the Military Intelligence Service (Abwehr).

Q. Which campaign is considered the greatest with regard to scope and number of personnel involved?

A. Operation Barbarossa, the German thrust to conquer Russia. Germany alone committed 300 divisions to it.

Q. Who commanded the Japanese Fourteenth Army that defended the Philippines from the U.S.?

A. General Tomoyuki Yamashita, Japan's most revered soldier.

Q. What was Karinhall?

A. Goering's palatial estate.

Q. How was Karinhall destroyed?

A. Before leaving for Hitler's birthday celebration on April 20, 1945, and only after a convoy of no fewer than twenty-four trucks had departed with his antiques, furniture, paintings, etc., the Reichsmarschall himself pushed the plunger destroying the estate. "Well, that's what you have to do sometimes when you're a crown prince," he told those around him. The Russians were expected to capture the area at any time.

Q. Which Allied airborne troops were considered expendable and actually had firecrackers attached to them set to explode upon landing during the D-Day invasion?

A. The hundreds of life-size rubber "paratrooper" dolls dropped to confuse the Germans.

Q. Who is credited with development of tanks as strategic war weapons?

A. General Heinz Guderian, who also created the blitzkrieg.

Q. How long did it take Germany to conquer France?

A. Twenty-seven days.

Q. How many rooms were in Hitler's bunker beneath the Chancellery in Berlin?

A. Including bathrooms, lounges in hallways, and storage areas, there were thirty-two rooms.

Q. Identify the first Allied troops to invade Fortress Europe by sea on D-Day.

A. At 4:30 A.M., 132 troops from the 4th and 24th U.S. Cavalry landed on the two rocky islands called Iles St. Marcouf, about three miles off Utah Beach, to destroy heavy gun emplacements that did not exist. Nor were there any enemy troops. However, nineteen men died in minefields.

Q. Identify any two of the Luftwaffe's five pilots who scored more than 250 "kills."

A. Erich Hartmann, 352
Gerhard Barkhorn, 301
Gunther Rall, 275
Otto Kittel, 267
Walter Nowotny, 255

FACT The allied air forces managed to overpower the German Luftwaffe not because heavy bombing had reduced the Reich's output of aircraft but because of a shortage of qualified German pilots. Overall armament production in Germany remained high until February 1944.

U.S. Army Photo

Q. How many days did the Germans occupy Paris?

A. From June 15, 1940, to August 25, 1944—1,524 days. During a 1940 visit to the city Hitler, center, took time to be photographed with his architect and armaments minister, Albert Speer (left), and sculptor Arno Breker. Breker, wearing an SS death's-head overseas cap, would later execute a larger-than-life marble bust of Hitler that Goering requested as a gift for his own birthday on January 12, 1944.

Q. Who replaced Montgomery as commander of the British Eighth Army when the hero of El Alamein was called to England in preparation for the D-Day invasion?

A. General Sir Oliver Leese.

Q. What was Dr. Joseph Goebbels' actual title?

A. Reichsminister for Public Enlightenment and Propaganda. In addition, he was the Gauleiter of Berlin.

Q. Name the American general who formally surrendered Bataan to the Japanese.

A. General Edward P. King, Jr., at 12:30 P.M. on April 9, 1942.

Q. What was the German *Fahneneid?*

A. The allegiance oath that the armed forces swore to the Fuehrer. Many officers who opposed Hitler felt they could not violate their oath.

Q. What was the name of the law that made the families of German generals responsible for the generals' actions?

A. Sippenschaft (apprehension and arrest of kin). After the plot to kill Hitler, SS Reichsleiter Robert Ley wrote the law. It was also designed to discourage surrender or failure to accomplish objectives. It was passed in August 1944.

Q. What was the Nazi Family Hostage Law?

A. An act by which all male relatives of an identified Resistance fighter would be executed. Female members of the family were sent to concentration camps, and children were placed in youth prisons. It was first issued in France on July 19, 1942. However, if the identified Resistance fighter surrendered, his family could escape the penalty.

FACT During what is known as the Battle of the Atlantic over 2,600 ships were sunk for a total of 15 million tons. Great Britain lost nearly 60,000 sailors and seamen. Germany lost 28,000 U-boat sailors and 785 submarines. U.S. losses were only a fraction of these.

Q. What was Hitler's infamous Commissar Order?

A. That all Soviet commissars captured were to be shot. The date was March 21, 1941, three months before Operation Barbarossa actually began.

Q. Which American unit made the greatest advances on D-Day?

A. The 4th Division, which moved inland from Utah Beach quicker than the most optimistic estimates.

Q. What did the initials CBI stand for with reference to a theater of operation?

A. The China-Burma-India Theater.

Q. What did Britain plan as the prelude to Operation Crusader, its counteroffensive against the Germans in North Africa?

A. The assassination of Erwin Rommel. Six officers and fifty-three commandos came ashore from the submarines *Torbay* and *Talisman*. Rommel's murder was one of four missions they were to execute. All were failures.

Q. What was *Der Weg zur Ewigkeit* (the Road to Eternity)?

A. The road between Berlin and Zossen, headquarters of the German High Command. Its official designation was Reichsstrasse 96.

Q. Identify the only father and son in the U.S. forces to have landed at Utah and Omaha beaches on June 6, 1944.

A. General Theodore Roosevelt, Jr., on Utah, and his son, Captain Quentin Roosevelt, on Omaha.

Q. Name the German allies who supplied fifty-two divisions for the 1942 summer offensive against Russia.

A. To reinforce its own troops Germany asked for, and got, Spanish, Hungarian, Slovakian, Italian and Rumanian divisions. Germany had lost 1.3 million troops in the first year of war with Russia.

Q. Which German army was responsible for the zone that included the five Normandy beaches where the Allies landed?

A. The Seventh Army, commanded by Colonel General Friedrich Dollmann. Because of bad weather he canceled a practice alert the night of June 5, 1944. For reasons never properly explained, this was the only German army not notified that intelligence knew the invasion was expected "within 48 hours."

Q. What was the largest U.S. land campaign of the war in the Pacific?

A. Lingayen Gulf and Luzon, where more U.S. troops than had participated in Italy or North Africa were involved.

Q. Identify the one-armed leader of the Hitler Youth.

A. Thirty-two-year-old Arthur Axmann, who ordered several hundred youngsters to resist the Russians to the death in the battle for Berlin. Nearly all obeyed.

Q. Which defeat resulted in the greatest U.S. surrender in history?

A. The Philippines in 1942.

Q. Identify the other three countries that participated in Operation Barbarossa with Germany against Russia.

A. Hungary, Rumania and Finland.

Q. Identify the Swedish Red Cross official that Heinrich Himmler secretly met with to discuss negotiating peace in April 1945.

A. Count Folke Bernadotte. The meetings were not successful.

Q. Who made the initial recommendation that Germany be divided into three sectors for occupation at the end of hostilities?

A. British Foreign Secretary, later Prime Minister, Anthony Eden in 1943.

Q. Identify the U.S. army charged with the assault on Salerno.

A. The U.S. Fifth Army, General Mark Clark commanding.

Q. Who was the head of the French underground army in 1944 prior to the liberation of Paris?

A. General Alfred Mallaret-Joinville, a communist.

Q. Identify the three countries occupied by U.S. Marines in the Atlantic.

A. On July 7, 1941, five months before its neutrality was to abruptly end, the U.S. Government occupied Trinidad, Iceland and British Guiana in order to free British troops for service elsewhere.

Agence France-Presse Photo

Q. Identify the Swedish consul general who arranged for the release of 532 political prisoners in Paris's Fresnes Prison in exchange for five times as many German POW's from the Allies as the Germans prepared to evacuate Paris.

A. Raoul Nordling, who was assisted by German Abwehr agent Emil Bender, an avid anti-Nazi. Nordling convinced Major Josef Huhm, chief of staff of the German occupation authority in France, that he could guarantee the deal. In fact Nordling had no authority, and he had no intention of seeing the swap accomplished by *both* sides.

Q. Who was commander-in-chief of the Polish Army when Germany invaded in 1939?

A. Marshal Edward Smigly-Rydz, who led an army capable of mustering 1,800,000 men. However, approximately 800,000 actually got to their divisions before the war in that country was over.

Q. Who was the British commander of the Army of the Nile when war in Europe broke out?

A. One-eyed General Sir Archibald Wavell.

Q. When did Field Marshal Erwin Rommel leave Africa for the last time?

A. On March 9, 1943. He was replaced by General Jurgen von Arnim. Rommel's last battle in Africa was on March 6, an offensive action against the British at Medenine that failed.

Q. At precisely what time on June 6, 1944, did the Allied invasion of Normandy begin?

A. At 12:15 A.M., when American and British Pathfinders dropped out of the sky to illuminate the way for the airborne divisions.

Q. Identify the American general criticized for taking too long to move off the beaches at Anzio before the Germans had a chance to mount a staunch defense?

A. Major General John P. Lucas of the U.S. VI Corps. He was replaced by Lieutenant General Lucian Truscott of the 3rd Division.

Q. Identify the Big Three heads of state who met in Cairo in November 1943.

A. Generalissimo Chiang Kai-shek of China joined President Roosevelt of the U.S. and Prime Minister Churchill of Great Britain.

FACT The greatest U.S. naval loss at sea was the July 30, 1945, sinking of the cruiser *Indianapolis* with a loss of nearly 900 men, mostly to sharks. The Japanese submarine I-58 scored with two torpedoes. It was the last major U.S. ship lost in the war. The *Indianapolis* was returning from delivering the uranium to Tinian Island that would be used in the first atom bombing of a Japanese city seven days later.

Q. Identify the hotel in Cairo where Churchill, Roosevelt and Chiang Kai-shek held their historic conference.

A. The Mena House, which is the closest hotel to the Pyramids of Giza. So close, in fact, that the distance can be walked in a short time.

Q. Identify the heads of state who participated in the Casablanca Conference.

A. President Roosevelt of the U.S. and Prime Minister Churchill of Great Britain. General Charles de Gaulle, who would eventually become Premier of France, was there also but not included in the major discussions.

Q. Who were the three world leaders in attendance at the Teheran Conference?

A. Once again President Roosevelt of the U.S. and Prime Minister Churchill of Great Britain were there, but this time Soviet Premier Joseph Stalin was also present.

Q. What was the task of the 813th Pionierkompanie of the Wehrmacht in Paris in August 1944?

A. Placing explosives at various bridges and monuments including the Eiffel Tower and Les Invalides. Hitler wanted the Allies to liberate ruins, not a city.

Q. Who was largely responsible for developing amphibious landing techniques in the Pacific?

A. Marine General Holland McTyeire Smith ("Howling Mad" Smith). He commanded the operations in the Gilbert and Marshall Islands, the Marianas and the Volcano Islands, from Tarawa to Iwo Jima.

FACT U.S. General George S. Patton became commander of the U.S. II Army Corps on the same day, March 6, 1943, that German Field Marshal Erwin Rommel began his last battle in North Africa. However, Patton turned command of the II Corps over to General Omar Bradley less than six weeks later. Patton was assigned to plan the Sicily invasion. Rommel had returned to Germany to defend against the expected Allied invasion of France.

French Tourist Office Photo

FACT: The world was horrified to learn that Hitler had ordered the beautiful bridges crossing the Seine destroyed as German troops withdrew from Paris. However, over seventy years earlier the French themselves passed laws installing special metal pans under *every* bridge in France for demolition purposes. The pans were designed to hold explosives so the French could destroy the bridges in a war emergency. The Germans in 1944 found the pans intact and prepared to use them. Above is a recent photo of Pont Alexander III, considered to be the most beautiful of the Seine bridges in Paris.

Q. What country did the members of Detachment 101 come from in the Burma campaign?

A. General Frank Merrill arranged for a tribe of Burmese natives, called Kachins, to participate in the struggle against the Japanese. The unit's war record reports killing 5,447 enemy and sustaining seventy Kachin and fifteen American losses.

Q. How many Allied personnel were evacuated during the nine days of Dunkirk?

A. There were 338,226 evacuated in more than a thousand boats of all shapes and sizes; 68,111 left behind were taken prisoner, wounded or killed.

Q. Who was the American commander during the battle for Cassino?

A. General Mark Clark, who was criticized for ordering the monastery bombed.

Q. When did the U.S. 36th Infantry Division make its combat debut?

A. The 36th Division, formerly the Texas National Guard, saw combat in World War II for the first time at Salerno, Italy.

Q. Where was the first British offensive in Southeast Asia?

A. On the Arakan coast of Burma on September 21, 1942.

Q. Identify the camp where the survivors of the Bataan Death March were imprisoned for the first three months.

A. Camp O'Donnell, some sixty miles from the Bataan Peninsula.

Q. Name the three Resistance political groups in Paris.

A. The three were the Paris Liberation Committee, the National Resistance Committee and the Military Action Committee.

Q. What was the overriding reason for the campaign to capture Guadalcanal?

A. The Japanese were building an air base that would threaten Australia with land-based bombers.

FACT The British 1st Airborne Division lost 75 percent of its personnel in the attack on Arnhem during Operation Market Garden.

Q. Which campaign is considered "the most spectacular series of victories ever gained over a British army"?

A. The German campaign to capture Tobruk in 1942, according to the history of the campaign as it is recorded in the official South African version.

Q. Identify the German general given the command of Army Group Vistula and ordered to hold the Russians on the Oder River as they attacked Berlin.

A. Colonel General Gotthard Heinrici, considered a brilliant defensive officer but disliked by Hitler for holding religious beliefs.

Q. Into what mountain was the tunnel fortress on Corregidor built?

A. Malinta Hill.

Q. Identify the SS general who met Allen Dulles of the OSS to try and negotiate peace in March 1945.

A. General Karl Wolff, smuggled into Zurich, Switzerland. He also met with General Lyman Lemnitzer on the same trip.

Q. What were U.S. Marine Corps casualties at Tarawa?

A. Eleven hundred. The Japanese lost over 4,600 troops, while only seventeen Japanese surrendered. In addition to the 1,100 U.S. troops killed, another 2,292 were wounded.

Q. Who did General Heinrici replace as commander of Army Group Vistula?

A. Reichsfuehrer Heinrich Himmler, who proved to be inept as a military commander and permitted himself to relinquish the post because of his other many jobs and his poor health. (Himmler was also Minister of the Interior, chief of the Gestapo, head of the SS and commander of the Training Army.)

Q. Identify the general who was commander-in-chief of the French Army when Germany invaded Poland.

A. General Maurice Gamelin. He was replaced by General Maxime Weygand on May 19, 1940, as a result of his inability to stop the German blitzkrieg.

Ullstein Photo

FACT: On the eve of the liberation of Paris Heinrich Himmler, seen here
shaking hands with Hitler, ordered a squad of SS to remove a particular tapestry from the Louvre. It depicted the invasion of England,
created nine centuries earlier for William the Conqueror. The Nazi
plan to invade England never came to pass, but Himmler thought the
tapestry would be appreciated by Hitler. The SS were unable to get
it, however, because of heavy fire from the French Resistance. Others
in photo, from left: Marshal Keitel, Admiral Doenitz, and Marshal
Milch.

Q. What was the name of the German intelligence organization that succeeded the Abwehr?

A. The Amt Mil.

Q. How long did it take for the Allies to recover from the German thrust in the Ardennes and push the Germans back behind their borders?

A. The recovery was rather swift, but it still took five weeks to recapture the lost ground.

Q. What is the historic significance of the British offensive against the Germans at El Agheila, Libya, on January 6, 1942?

A. It marked the first British victory over the Germans in the war. The British Eighth Army caused nearly 40,000 German casualties.

Q. Who was SS Gruppenfuehrer Heinrich Muller?

A. The head of the Gestapo, under Himmler.

Q. What was the German paramilitary construction organization called that included both engineers and workers.

A. The Todt Organization.

Q. When did the last Polish troops surrender after the German invasion?

A. On September 17, 1939, about 52,000 Polish troops surrendered at Warsaw. The last organized Polish resistance was southeast of Warsaw, at Kock, which surrendered on October 6. Approximately 17,000 Poles were involved.

Q. Which U.S. unit spearheaded the Sicily invasion?

A. The 505th Parachute Regimental Combat Team, on July 9, 1943. It was part of the 82nd Airborne Division.

FACT General Joseph Stilwell served as chief of staff to Supreme Commander Chiang Kai-shek in China, commander of U.S. forces in the China-Burma-India theater, and subordinate to the British commander in India, all at the same time. This made him responsible to Washington, China and London simultaneously.

Q. Identify the first three U.S. generals to land during the Normandy invasion in 1944.

A. The first three were Matthew B. Ridgway, 82nd Airborne; Maxwell D. Taylor, 101st Airborne; and James M. Gavin, 82nd Airborne, pictured here.

Q. Name the location in the Middle East where Free French and Vichy French troops fought each other, and when did it happen?

A. In June 1941 in Vichy French Syria. The British felt if they employed Free French units the Vichy troops would be reluctant to kill other Frenchmen. Units of the Free French that General de Gaulle consigned to the Middle East Command were used. The British were wrong, and several Frenchmen on both sides died before the Vichy French surrendered.

Q. Identify any three of the multinational armies General Alexander commanded in the battle for Cassino.

A. They included a brigade of Palestinian Jews, Poles, Moroccans, Greeks, Senegalese, Italians, Algerians, Brazilians, Indians, South Africans, Canadians, French, New Zealanders, British and Americans.

Q. Who was Hitler's personal bodyguard in the last days of the war?

A. SS Colonel Otto Gunsche.

Q. How many hours after General MacArthur had been notified of the Pearl Harbor attack was Manila attacked?

A. Between eight and nine hours. Yet, as at air bases at Pearl Harbor, his planes remained on the ground and were easy targets.

Q. Who was the head of German Military Intelligence (Abwehr) in France in 1944?

A. Colonel Friedrich Garthe.

Q. What do the initials COSSAC stand for?

A. Chief of Staff, Supreme Allied Commander.

Q. Why did Canada wait seven days, until September 10, 1939, to follow Britain, Australia, New Zealand and India in declaring war on Germany?

A. Because Canada was expecting large shipments of war materiel from the U.S. The U.S., which was neutral, could not send such materiel to a belligerent. The delay permitted the delivery.

Q. Who became German Fuehrer upon the death of Hitler?

A. Admiral Karl Doenitz.

Q. Identify the town in Sicily that Patton raced and beat Montgomery to.

A. After conquering most of the island, including Palermo, Patton captured Messina, which had been Montgomery's objective, and he delighted in welcoming the field marshal upon his late arrival.

Q. What was the area of beachhead involved in the Normandy landings?

A. Approximately sixty miles along the Cotentin Peninsula.

Q. What German general was responsible for creating a limited scorched-earth plan to be used as the Germans withdrew from Paris?

A. Generalleutnant Gunther Blumentritt, chief of staff to Generalfeldmarschall Gunther von Kluge, commander of OB West (Oberbefehlshaber West).

Q. How long did it take Germany to conquer Belgium?

A. Seventeen days.

Q. How long did the Dutch hold out against the German invasion?

A. Five days.

Q. What was the ABDA Command?

A. The short-lived effort that combined American, British, Dutch and Australian forces in the Pacific. Each nation had its own idea of what the ABDA should do; as a result it was terminated after less than two months in the early part of 1942.

Q. What was the function of the London Controlling Section (LCS)?

A. Created by Winston Churchill, its purpose was to deceive the Germans about Allied plans and operations through the use of stratagems, lies and misleading acts.

FACT Italy signed two documents marking its end of participation in the war as a member of the Axis. The first, on September 3, 1943, was not publicly announced, in order to avoid a German move at seizing control of the country. The second, public announcement came five days later.

Q. Which high-ranking Nazi claimed he told Hitler to end the war three times and even considered murdering Hitler?

A. Albert Speer said he brought the subject up in October 1944 and again in January and March of 1945. He told General Gotthard Heinrici, commander of Army Group Vistula, that he had considered introducing poison gas into the ventilating system of the Fuehrerbunker. During the meeting with Heinrici, Speer produced a pistol, saying it was "the only way to stop Hitler." But Speer never attempted an assassination.

Q. Identify the U.S. Marine commander of the Guadalcanal invasion.

A. Major General Alexander A. Vandergrift of the 1st Marine Division.

Q. Identify the Norwegian location where the Germans produced heavy water for atomic research.

A. Rjukan. From there it was sent to the Kaiser Wilhelm Institute for research in Germany.

Q. Besides Hitler, his new wife Eva Braun, and Joseph and Magda Goebbels, identify some of the other people who committed suicide in the bunker.

A. OKH chief of staff, General Hans Krebs; Hitler's adjutant, General Wilhelm Burgdorf; and Captain Franz Schedle of the SS bunker guards.

Q. Where was Bloody Nose Ridge?

A. On Peleliu, in the Pacific. It took Marine and Army personnel one month to capture the island from the Japanese. More than 11,000 Japanese were killed by the attacking force of 45,000 Americans.

Q. Which British unit went into battle on D-Day accompanied by wailing bagpipes?

A. The 1st Special Service Brigade commandos under Lord Lovat. The piper was William Millin, who played "Blue Bonnets over the Border" more than once that day.

Q. How many concentration camps did the Nazis operate in Germany and occupied countries?

A. More than thirty, of which Auschwitz, Buchenwald, Belsen, Dachau and Ravensbruck were the most infamous.

Q. Identify the U.S. Marine Corps general who commanded the V Marines in the invasion of Iwo Jima.

A. Major General Harry Schmidt.

Q. Who had the distinction of announcing officially to the world that the Allies had invaded France on D-Day?

A. Colonel Ernest Dupuy, press aide to the Supreme Allied Commander. It was announced at 9:30 A.M. June 6, 1944.

Q. Name the "impregnable" fort in Belgium that the Germans captured in thirty hours?

A. Fort Eben Emael. German paratroopers had trained in advance of the attack at a replica. One sergeant and eighty men assaulted and captured it.

Q. Which two U.S. generals threatened to quit if Eisenhower appointed Montgomery Land Forces Commander?

A. Omar Bradley and George Patton. Monty had sought the role more than once, but Ike refused to relinquish command. Monty believed so strongly in the post, however, he once offered to serve subordinate to Bradley.

Q. Identify the German gun introduced in the North African campaign that sliced through British armor almost effortlessly?

A. The 88 millimeter.

Q. How many anti-personnel and anti-marine mines and obstacles had the Germans laced the European shoreline with in hopes of foiling the D-Day landings?

A. There were reportedly over a half million lethal devices awaiting Allied troops.

Q. What was the obvious difference between U.S. Army A rations and C and K rations?

A. A rations indicated the meal was prepared in an area where it could be refrigerated and was, as a result, better than the K or C rations. C rations included Spam and nine other meat compounds, dehydrated eggs and potatoes and an assortment of other "almost foods."

Q. How did the German S mines react when stepped on?

A. They snapped into the air and detonated at the victim's midriff.

Q. Name the German commanding general of Paris who failed to follow Hitler's orders and destroy the city.

A. General Dietrich von Choltitz, commandant of Festung Paris (Fortress Paris), delayed giving the order that would have set off explosions in a number of architectural treasures, including the Eiffel Tower, because he didn't want to be remembered in history with that stigma. Because the city was liberated without the destruction Hitler wished, Choltitz was tried in absentia for treason by a Nazi court in April 1945. The order to destroy Paris had been given on August 23, 1944.

Q. Name the Japanese commander who defeated MacArthur's army in the Philippines.

A. Lieutenant General Masahara Homma, who was executed after the war for his role in the Death March at Bataan.

Q. Identify the German city that was the target of the first thousand-bomber raid in the war.

A. Cologne, on May 30–31, 1942. The RAF air armada took off from fifty-two airfields in Britain.

Q. What was the significance of the London *Daily Telegraph*'s crossword puzzles in May and June 1944?

A. Several of the answers turned out to be code names for the Normandy invasion. From May 2 through early June compiler Leonard Sideny Dawe coincidentally used Overlord, Utah, Omaha, Mulberry, Neptune and others.

Q. Who created the comic character Sad Sack, and where did it first appear?

A. U.S. Army Sergeant George Baker created him, and millions of servicemen followed Sad Sack adventures in *Yank* magazine.

FACT   The Allies used more than 10,000 code names for various persons, places and operations during the war.

U.S. Army Photo

Q. Who created "Willie and Joe," and where did the cartoon appear?

A. Bill Mauldin's two hapless GI's were found in the pages of the U.S. military newspaper *Stars and Stripes*. The best antics of Willie and Joe appeared in Mauldin's postwar book *Up Front*. Photo above shows some of the 15,000 copies of the extra edition of the paper that came off the presses of *The Times* of London on May 7, 1945. *Stars and Stripes* was the first newspaper to hit the London streets with the full story of the German surrender.

Q. What was the name of the official Nazi Party newspaper in Berlin?

A. *Voelkischer Beobachter.*

Q. Identify the trio of newspapers in Paris that collaborated with the Germans.

A. The three were a weekly, *Je Suis Partout,* and two dailies, *Le Petit Parisien* and *Paris-Soir.*

Q. What was the name of the Nazi newspaper that Propaganda Minister Goebbels had published during the last six days before Berlin surrendered?

A. *Der Panzerbar (The Armored Bear),* which was intended to raise morale among the citizens defending the city against the Russians. The more famous Nazi newspaper *Voelkischer Beobachter* had been the last of Berlin's regular newspapers to cease publishing.

Q. What was the name of the German-language newspaper printed in Paris during the German occupation?

A. *Pariser Zeitung,* which ceased to go to bed in August 1944 after 221 editions.

Q. What was the headline in the *Atlanta Constitution* on President Roosevelt's desk when he died on April 12, 1945, at Warm Springs, Georgia?

A. "9th 57 Miles from Berlin," which reported the progress of the U.S. Ninth Army.

Q. Name the three Resistance newspapers in Paris that began publishing in August 1944.

A. The three were *Libération, Le Parisien Libéré* and *Défense de la France.*

Q. Which newsman broke the story about General Patton slapping a shell-shocked soldier?

A. Drew Pearson. Although other correspondents agreed not to file the stories about two separate incidents, Pearson did not feel so obligated.

Q. Identify the future U.S. senator who was sued by Adolf Hitler for copyright infringement over *Mein Kampf.*

A. Alan Cranston (D., Calif.), who after reading both the original in German and the U.S. version decided too much had been edited out and promptly published *Adolf Hitler's Own Book*. Cranston was a news correspondent at the time in the 1930s, and the book sold a half million copies before a U.S. injunction forced him to discontinue offering it.

Q. Who was Adolf Hitler's German publisher?

A. Max Amann, an early Nazi and friend.

Q. Who actually made Winston Churchill's famous "We shall fight on the beaches" speech on the BBC in June 1940?

A. Churchill made the speech in Parliament but permitted actor Norman Shelley to re-create it on the air, as the PM was busy with the evacuation of Dunkirk. Shelley's imitation was good enough to fool Churchill's closest friends. It is the only time the PM permitted such an act.

Q. Identify the U.S. newsman who made the last broadcast from Paris before the German occupation in 1940.

A. Larry Lesueur of CBS, on June 10, which was his thirtieth birthday. Lesueur also has the distinction of making the first broadcast out of liberated Paris on August 25, 1944.

Q. How did the premature message of the liberation of Paris come to be broadcast?

A. CBS newsman Charles Collingwood had recorded the story in advance and forwarded it to London for use at the appropriate time. However a mixup resulted in it being broadcast on August 23, two full days before the actual liberation. It was carried throughout the world.

Q. In what languages did the BBC broadcast coded messages after the regular news?

A. French, Norwegian, Dutch and Danish.

Q. What radio station did Allied troops tune in when they wanted to hear the latest hits after the D-Day landing?

A. Radio Paris and the sexy-voiced Axis Sally.

FACT: The two most recognizable voices Americans heard on their radios broadcasting from London belonged to Winston Churchill and Edward R. Murrow, above. The dapper Murrow was not above lying in the gutter so that his microphone could pick up the sounds of bombs and sirens. By the time this 1941 photo was made, he was already a legend in broadcasting. By the end of the war Murrow had flown as an observer on twenty-five combat missions. His CBS broadcasts from England opened with "This . . . is London."

Q. What were the British islands that came under the control of an Axis power?

A. The Channel Islands, which had fallen to the Germans at the end of June 1940 and were not liberated until May 9, 1945. They are approximately eighty miles off the southern English coast and some forty miles from Cherbourg, France.

Q. Identify the last European capital to be liberated in May 1945.

A. Prague, Czechoslovakia, by the Russians.

Q. Identify the Yugoslav monarch deposed by Tito when the Partisan resistance leader declared the People's Republic of Yugoslavia?

A. King Peter II on November 23, 1943.

Q. Identify the Associated Press newsman who was ordered to leave the European theater of war for scooping the world with the news that the Germans had surrendered.

A. Edward Kennedy earned that distinction for his violation of the official release time when he broke the story on May 7, 1945.

Q. Name the only two countries whose declarations of war against the U.S. were not "accepted."

A. During the month of December 1941, diplomatic exchanges of declarations of war between Allied and Axis powers and various sympathizers were relatively rapid and, obviously, accepted. However, the U.S. refused to accept the Slovakia declaration on December 12, and then on the 14th refused to accept the Croat declaration against the U.S.

Q. Name the only bridge in Florence, Italy, that was not destroyed by the retreating Germans in August 1944.

A. The historic fourteenth-century Ponte Vecchio.

Q. Identify the three former French premiers who were liberated by U.S. troops from confinement in Austria in May 1945.

A. The three were Edouard Daladier, Paul Reynaud and Léon Blum. In addition, former Austrian Chancellor Kurt von Schuschnigg and French generals Weygand and Gamelin were also liberated.

Q. Who was the commanding Japanese general of the Okinawa defense against the Americans in 1945?

A. Lieutenant General Mitsuru Ushijima, who committed suicide on June 22, 1945, and became one of the approximately 110,000 Japanese who died during the eighty-one-day conflict. U.S. Marine and Army losses were 12,520 killed and over 36,000 wounded.

Q. When was Athens free of German troops?

A. The Germans began to withdraw on October 2, 1944, and were completely out by October 14, the same day British troops landed on the island of Corfu.

Q. Identify the U.S. Marine Corps division that established the first beachhead on Peleliu Island on September 15, 1944.

A. The 1st Marine Division, in a campaign where progress was gauged in yards, sometimes feet. The U.S. Army sent troops from the 81st Division to assist the Marines on September 23. The island was not secured until October 14.

Q. What was the last major amphibious operation of the war?

A. The invasion of Okinawa. About 60,000 U.S. troops (two Marine and two Army divisions) were involved.

Q. Identify the U.S. troops that invaded the island of Ie-shima during the Okinawa campaign.

A. The U.S. 77th Division assaulted the island on April 16, 1945.

Q. Identify the German city near a salt mine where U.S. troops uncovered a tremendous amount of buried Nazi treasure.

A. When the U.S. 90th Division captured Merkers, they discovered art, gold and other valuables (much of which was Nazi plunder from occupied countries) buried in the nearby salt mine. The discovery was in April 1945.

FACT Rommel and his army were surrounded by German troops on September 15, 1939, and ordered to surrender. He declined the offer. However, Major General Juliusz Rommel was the military commander of Warsaw, not the German general and future field marshal of North Africa fame.

U.S. Coast Guard Photo

FACT: U.S. war correspondent Ernie Pyle covered the war in both the Atlantic and Pacific theaters. After he was killed, one of his manuscripts was auctioned for over $10 million during a War Bond drive in Indianapolis, Indiana. Sharing a cup of coffee somewhere in the Pacific, en route to the Ryukus, are Pyle and U.S. Coast Guard commander, former heavyweight boxing champion of the world, Jack Dempsey.

Q. Identify the Japanese Army major that led the abortive attempt to stage a coup in Tokyo during April 1945 when he learned that the Emperor had prepared a surrender speech.

A. Though Japan would not surrender for over four months, Major Kenji Hatanaka and other officers could not even consider the possibility. When the April 14–15 plot failed, Hatanaka committed suicide.

Q. Identify the three countries Germany invaded on May 10, 1940.

A. The three were Belgium, Holland and Luxembourg.

Q. Identify the first country to join the original Axis powers of Germany, Japan and Italy.

A. Bulgaria, on March 1, 1941.

Q. Identify the neutral country that had an official two-day mourning period after the death of Adolf Hitler.

A. Portugal, where flags were flown at half staff on April 30 and May 1, 1945. Another country that followed diplomatic protocol was Ireland. Prime Minister Eamon de Valera actually expressed his condolences to German representatives in Dublin on May 2, 1945.

Q. Identify the location that has the distinction of being the only North American territory occupied by an Axis power during the war.

A. The Aleutian Islands, where a Japanese invasion force of approximately 1,800 troops landed unopposed on June 7, 1942, on Attu and Kiska.

Q. Name the German general who because of his ability to always agree with Hitler and seek approval was called "Lackey" by other army officers.

A. Field Marshal Wilhelm Keitel, Chief of the Supreme Command of the German Armed Forces. A little wordplay with his name changed it to *Lakeitel,* which in German means "lackey."

FACT   The total number of aircraft used by both sides during the war was approximately 675,000 planes, of which 475,000 were employed by the Allies.

Q. When was the American flag raised on Iwo Jima?

A. February 23, 1945. The invasion began February 19, the battle lasted twenty-six days.

Q. Who provided the flag that was raised on Mount Suribachi, Iwo Jima?

A. The first flag, a small one that a U.S. Marine had brought with him and lashed to an iron pipe, was replaced by the battle ensign from LST-779 down on the beach. This is the flag in the famous Associated Press photo by Joe Rosenthal.

Q. Name the servicemen who raised the flag on Iwo Jima.

A. The *first* flag-raising on Mount Suribachi was by Marines H. O. Hansen, E. I. Thomas, H. B. Shrier, J. R. Michaels and C. W. Lindberg. It is recorded in U.S. Navy Photo 304841.

Q. Where was the closest American flag to the Japanese homeland raised during combat?

A. On the northern end of Okinawa in mid-April 1945 by the U.S. 6th Marine Division. They also raised the same flag on the southern end of the island on June 21.

Q. Identify the military unit that was the first to occupy Japan.

A. The U.S. 4th Marines.

Q. What two teams were playing a football game at the Polo Grounds in New York when the broadcast was interrupted with the news of the Pearl Harbor attack?

A. The Dodgers and the Giants. Ward Cuff of the Giants had caught a Dodger kickoff and brought it to the Giants' twenty-seven-yard line. It was 2:26 P.M., and radio station WOR broadcast the news that the Japanese had attacked the U.S. Naval Base at Pearl Harbor in Hawaii.

FACT Claus von Bulow, the Rhode Island financier who on March 16, 1982, was convicted of twice trying to kill his heiress wife with insulin injections so he could collect a $14 million inheritance and marry his mistress, had been a page at the wedding of Reichsmarschall Hermann Goering in the 1930s.

Q. Name the Australian Prime Minister who died in July 1945 after leading his country since 1941.

A. John Curtin. His passing marked the fourth death of a head of state of a major World War II combatant in three months. Roosevelt, Mussolini and Hitler had preceded him.

Q. What was the only industry that provided its products free of charge to the U.S. Government throughout the war?

A. The film industry. Prints of all features were provided at no cost for entertainment of servicemen. Over 43,000 prints were furnished.

Q. Where did the U.S. Army get its first taste of combat against the Germans?

A. At Kasserine Pass, Tunisia, against Rommel's Afrika Korps, which had created a bulge in Allied lines. About 2,400 inexperienced U.S. troops surrendered.

FACT   The most decorated World War II veteran ever elected to Congress was Sen. Daniel Ken Inouye (D-Hawaii) who was awarded the Distinguished Service Medal, Bronze Star, Purple Heart with clusters, and five Battle Stars. Inouye is a third-generation American whose ancestry is Japanese.

The Air War

Q. Who was the ace of aces among all the combatant nations in the war?

A. Luftwaffe Major Erich Hartmann, with 352 "kills." Several German pilots recorded over 100 "kills," and five had more than 250. This was due in part to the fact that they did not rotate tours of duty with rest periods as the Allies did, and they counted aircraft shot on the ground.

Q. Who won fame in the Battle of Britain as the "legless air ace"?

A. Squadron Leader Douglas Bader, who lost both legs in a crash in 1931. In 1939, wearing artificial legs, he rejoined the service. He is credited with twenty-three "kills."

Q. What was the name of the airfield the U.S. Marines built on Guadalcanal?

A. Henderson Field, after Major Loften R. Henderson of the Midway-based Marine Aircraft Group, who was killed during the Battle of Midway. They used abandoned Japanese equipment to convert a level piece of ground that the Japanese had cleared for use as an airstrip.

Q. Identify the bombsight that is credited with much of the success the U.S. had in precision bombing.

A. The Norden.

U.S. Navy Photo

Q. Identify the major Midwestern U.S. city that named an airport in honor of the first U.S. Navy ace of the war.

A. Chicago, the Windy City, named O'Hare Airport for Lieutenant Edward "Butch" O'Hare, who downed five Japanese planes on February 20, 1942. O'Hare was stationed on the aircraft carrier *Lexington*. While flying from the *Enterprise* during activity in the Central Pacific in 1944 he lost his life. His 1942 combat action won him the Congressional Medal of Honor.

Q. How did the Japanese get aerial photos of Hickam Field and Pearl Harbor?

A. By having agents take private sightseeing plane rides from John Rogers Airport. Their task was duplicated hundreds of times by ordinary tourists.

Q. Identify the aircraft considered by many to have been the best torpedo bomber of the war.

A. The Italian Savoia-Marchetti Sparviero, which was called the Damned Hunchback. It was also used as a transport and reconnaissance plane. More than half of the Italian Air Force's bombers were Damned Hunchbacks.

Q. Who was Britain's top ace, including pilots from throughout the Commonwealth?

A. Major Saint John Pattle from South Africa with forty-one "kills."

Q. Identify the pilot who flew more combat missions than anyone else in the war.

A. Luftwaffe ace Hans-Ulrich Rudel. According to German records, he flew 2,530 combat missions. He is the only German ever awarded a Knight's Cross to the Iron Cross with Golden Oak Leaves and Swords and Diamonds, the second highest degree of Iron Cross. (The highest degree is Great Cross of the Iron Cross, which was also only awarded once, to Hermann Goering.)

Q. Name the other three Japanese cities bombed at the time of Doolittle's raid on Tokyo in April 1942.

A. Kobe, Nagoya and Yokohama were the three.

Q. How many women served as pilots in the Soviet Air Force?

A. More than 5,000, of whom Lieutenant Lilya Litvak with seven "kills" and Lieutenant Katya Budanova with six "kills" were the top two fighter aces.

FACT The wearing of Star of David cloth identification badges for Polish Jews began on November 23, 1939, less than three months after the war began. The order was extended to Jews in all Baltic States on July 8, 1941.

Q. Who founded the Free French Air Force?

A. General Charles de Gaulle.

Q. Identify the two aircraft involved in the last dogfight in the European theater.

A. A Piper Cub unarmed spotting plane named *Miss Me* of the U.S. 5th Armored and a German Fieseler Storch, also a spotting plane, met in the sky over Germany in April 1945. Lieutenant Duane Francies, pilot, and his observer, Lieutenant William Martin, dove on the Storch and fired their .45 Colts, bringing the German plane down. They landed and captured the pilot and German observer. It was the only German plane shot down with a handgun.

Q. Who was the American Army Air Force officer that Reichsmarschall Hermann Goering offered a $5,000 reward for?

A. Tail gunner Clark Gable, who may or may not have quipped after hearing it, "Frankly, Herr Reichsmarschall, I don't give a damn!"

Q. Where did the Japanese introduce the kamikaze plane?

A. The Battle for Leyte Gulf. In Japanese, *kamikaze* means "divine wind" and refers to the typhoon that struck the invading Mongol fleet prepared to invade Japan in the Middle Ages.

Q. What was the name of the B-29 that dropped the second atomic bomb on a Japanese city? Name the city and when it was done.

A. On August 9, 1945, Major Charles W. Sweeney diverted his plane, named *Bock's Car,* from its primary target, Kokura, and bombed the secondary target, Nagasaki. The plane, along with the *Enola Gay,* was part of the 509th Composite Group, 313th Wing, of the Twentieth U.S. Air Force.

Q. Which English ace earned the best record?

A. Captain James E. Johnson, with thirty-eight "kills."

Q. What was the name of Adolf Hitler's pilot?

A. Hans Baur.

Q. Identify the only Rumanian-built fighter plane to see action during the war.

A. The I.A.R. 80. Production began in 1941.

Q. After the famous raid on Tokyo by Lieutenant Colonel James Doolittle, when was the next time U.S. bombers attacked Japan?

A. Not until more than two years later, on June 15, 1944. This time B-29s from a base in China dropped 221 tons of bombs on the Yawata ironworks on the island of Kyushu.

Q. Identify the all-female fighter group in the Soviet Air Force.

A. The 586th Fighter Aviation Regiment, 122nd Air Division, which flew more than 4,400 combat missions.

Q. Identify the aircraft considered the best French fighter of the war.

A. The Dewoitine D-520. France had only produced thirty-six of them that were in service before the armistice with Germany. Under occupation, approximately 870 were produced for use by the Luftwaffe and the Italians, Bulgarians and Rumanians.

Q. What is considered the most significant result of the Battle of the Bismarck Sea with regard to air power?

A. The fact that the Japanese troop convoy heading for New Guinea with reinforcements was wiped out, and more than 6,000 troops and 102 planes were destroyed. The U.S. Fifth Air Force was under the command of Major General George C. Kenny.

Q. Identify the two types of RAF planes credited with winning the Battle of Britain.

A. The Spitfire and the Hurricane.

Q. Identify the first type of monoplane fighter to operate from a U.S. aircraft carrier.

A. The Brewster Buffalo.

Q. Which aircraft was the first monoplane deck fighter in the Japanese navy?

A. The Mitsubishi A5M4, produced in 1937 and taken out of service in 1942. The Allied code name was Claude.

Q. Which aircraft holds the distinction of being the first monoplane used by the RAF?

A. The Avro Anson. It was also the first aircraft in RAF service to boast retractable landing gear.

U.S. Navy Photo

Q. Who was the U.S. Army Air Force commander in Hawaii on December 7, 1941:

        a. William Farthing
        b. Frederick L. Martin
        c. William W. Outerbridge

A. General Frederick L. Martin. Colonel William Farthing was commander of Hickam Field and Lieutenant William W. Outerbridge was the skipper of the U.S. destroyer *Ward,* the ship that sank the first ship at Pearl Harbor, a Japanese midget submarine. A destroyed U.S. B-17 sits on the runway at Hickam in this photo.

Q. Name the Australian-built fighter plane that was designed and (a prototype) built in four weeks.

A. The CA-12 Boomerang. Because of the difficulty in obtaining U.S. or British aircraft to fend off the Japanese, the Australians instantly created one of their own. A total of 250 Boomerang fighters were produced.

Q. Who was the leading Irish ace fighting for Britain?

A. Colonel Brendan E. Finucane, who is credited with thirty-two "kills."

Q. Identify the well-known German aviatrix who landed a Fieseler Storch in the heart of Berlin during the height of the battle for the city.

A. Hanna Reitsch, who had taken over the controls from General Ritter von Greim, wounded in the approach. They had been called to Berlin by Hitler.

Q. When did U.S. personnel participate as full crews for the first time in a bombing mission over occupied Europe?

A. On July 4, 1942, U.S.-crewed planes joined an RAF raid on Luftwaffe airfields in Holland. The U.S. lost two of the six planes that participated.

Q. Other than British, which nations had the greatest and which had the least number of squadrons in the RAF by the time the Allies invaded France?

A. There were forty-two Canadian squadrons, the most, and one Yugoslav squadron among the 487 in the RAF. A total of 157 squadrons in the RAF were international by D-Day.

Q. Name the aircraft that was the backbone of the Polish Air Force when the Germans invaded.

A. Poland had 125 P.Z.L. P-11c aircraft, first produced in 1933, as her total fighter plane power in September 1939. For seventeen days these outdated planes engaged in more modern aircraft of the Luftwaffe before the surrender. Only seven were left at the end, but they had shot down 126 German aircraft.

Q. Identify the type of U.S. aircraft that the Japanese nicknamed Whistling Death.

A. The Chance-Vought F4U-1 Corsair, which went into service in 1943. It is credited with more than 2,000 successful missions.

Q. Identify the Japanese jet-engine air bomb piloted by a kamikaze pilot and carried by a larger plane to its target.

A. The Yokosuka MXY7, code-named Baka by the Allies. Japan produced five versions and a total of 852 of these suicide bombs.

Q. Identify the Italian plane that participated in the Battle of Britain with the Germans and was also used by the Japanese against the Chinese.

A. The Fiat Cicogna light bomber. Italian pilots flew them over Britain, but in China the pilots were Japanese. Tokyo purchased seventy-five Cicognas from Italy in 1938.

Q. Identify the top Canadian ace of the war.

A. Major George F. Beurling, with thirty-one "kills."

Q. Who was the immediate object of Rudolf Hess's flight to Britain?

A. The Duke of Hamilton, whom he had met at the 1936 Olympics and hoped would deliver him to Britain's leaders to discuss peace.

Q. How many U.S. military aircraft from all services were based on Oahu on December 7, 1941? How many got aloft?

A. Of the approximately 390 aircraft at various bases, thirty-eight got into the sky, and ten of these were shot down.

Q. Which country developed the first single-engine low-wing fighter plane that had retractable landing gear?

A. The Soviet Union developed the Polikarpov, which was known as the Rata during the Spanish Civil War.

Q. Who was France's top ace?

A. Pierre Closterman, with thirty-three "kills." He rose from the rank of sergeant to major in the Free French Air Force, which was based in England.

Q. Identify the only Allied jet aircraft to enter service during the war.

A. The Gloster Meteor III, which made its inaugural flight on March 5, 1943, but didn't face enemy aircraft until July 1944. They actually faced V-1 bombs but not piloted planes.

Q. What type Allied aircraft is credited with scoring the first "kill" against a German plane?

A. A Lockheed A-29 Hudson, American made, but in service for the British Coastal Command. A Hudson was also the first American plane to sink a German U-boat.

Q. What was the proper name of the most famous Japanese aircraft produced during the war?

A. The Mitsubishi A6M3 Zero, which was known to the Allies as Zeke. Japan manufactured 10,449 of them, including 465 modified versions as kamikazes.

Q. Who was Italy's top air ace of the war?

A. Major Adriano Visconti, with twenty-six "kills." Despite Italy's inferior air power due to lack of aircraft, its pilots were considered among the finest in the war.

Q. Identify the first German city to suffer a bombing raid in the war.

A. On September 4, 1939, the RAF bombed Brunsbüttelkoog.

Q. Identify the type of fighter plane General Claire Chennault's Flying Tigers used.

A. The Curtis P-40 Warhawk. In England it was called the Tomahawk and the Kittyhawk.

Q. Who was the Soviet air ace of aces?

A. Colonel Ivan N. Kozhedub, with sixty-two "kills."

Q. What was the name of the Free French fighter group that fought in Russia with the 1st Soviet Air Division?

A. Normandie, which functioned from early 1943 on. Four members of this group were honored as Heroes of the Soviet Union. Each had over ten "kills" to his credit.

Q. Where and when did the RAF and the Luftwaffe first meet in air combat?

A. Over Aachen on September 20, 1939, when the Germans shot down two enemy planes and the British scored one enemy plane. Aircraft involved were Messerschmitts and Battles.

Q. Where did the four dive-bombers that were accidentally shot down trying to land at Pearl Harbor come from on the night of December 7, 1941?

A. The carrier *Enterprise.* They had landed earlier in the day but had been sent out to search for the Japanese fleet. Returning in the dark, they were mistaken for enemy planes.

Q. Who was Japan's ace of aces in the war?

A. Hiroyishi Nishizawa with 87 "kills."

Q. What plane was the first all-metal fighter produced by Italy?

A. The Fiat G-50 Freccia, designed in 1937. Used in the Spanish Civil War on a limited basis, the Freccia saw action in Greece, Belgium, Libya, the Balkans and the Aegean Sea. Approximately 675 were manufactured.

Q. Identify the type of RAF plane that dropped the first 8,000-pound bomb on Germany.

A. A Halifax, the night of April 10–11, 1942.

Q. When did U.S. aircraft participate in the first totally American air raid on Germany?

A. On January 27, 1943, bombing the German port of Wilhelmshaven.

Q. How much were the American volunteers in Chennault's Flying Tigers paid for their participation in China?

A. They earned $600 per month plus $500 for each "kill."

Q. Did the French Air Force ever actually bomb a German city during its brief combat service in the war?

A. Yes, Berlin, on June 7, 1940.

Q. What were the names of the three old Gladiator biplanes that defended Malta from the Germans?

A. *Faith, Hope* and *Charity.*

FACT In the early offensives of the North African campaign most of Rommel's troops were Italian.

Q. Who was America's ace of aces?

A. Major Richard I. Bong, forty "kills."

Q. What was the largest flying boat produced during the war?

A. The German Blohn & Voss Bv222C Wiking. Designed in 1940 by Lufthansa for use in passenger service across the Atlantic, these huge six-engine aircraft were put to military use in September 1941 as troop and materiel transports. Fourteen were manufactured.

Q. What was the first Japanese heavy bomber to have a tail-gun turret?

A. The Nakajimi Ki-49-II, code-named Helen by the Allies. Just over 800 were manufactured. It first saw combat on February 19, 1942, in the bombing of Port Darwin, Australia.

Q. Identify the Italian city that was the object of the first RAF daylight raid from British bases.

A. Milan, on October 24, 1942. The trip was just over 2,800 air miles.

Q. What city was the target of the most destructive RAF air raid of the war?

A. Hamburg, Germany, on July 27–28, 1943, when nearly 750 RAF bombers dropped over 2,400 tons of bombs, many of which were incendiaries that created fire storms with winds of over 150 miles per hour. Official records put the death toll at 20,000 and the injured at more than 60,000.

Q. Who was Australia's top ace?

A. Captain Clive R. Caldwell, twenty-eight "kills."

Q. How many aircraft did the Luftwaffe use in the Battle of Britain?

A. They used 3,550, including 2,000 bombers.

FACT Anti-Hitler German officers tried and failed twice to kill Hitler during one week in March 1943. In the second attempt Colonel Rudolph von Gertsdorff had to flush the fuse of a bomb down a toilet when Hitler left a meeting before the bomb could be detonated. The incident took place at the Zeughaus exhibition hall in Berlin.

Q. What was the Central Aircraft Manufacturing Company (CAMCO)?

A. The cover name for the American volunteer organization General Claire L. Chennault recruited to fight the Japanese for China. The fighting units were called the American Volunteer Group (AVG) when they began training in September 1941. After Pearl Harbor they became a legend as the Flying Tigers.

Q. What was the strength of the French Armée de l'Air (Air Force) when war began?

A. Counting those attached to French colonies, there were 3,600 aircraft. Only 1,400, however, were in the mother country.

Q. What were the strengths of the RAF and the Luftwaffe at the start of the Battle of Britain?

A. The RAF had 704 serviceable aircraft vs. 2,682 for the Luftwaffe.

Q. What was the fastest propeller fighter plane ever built?

A. The U.S.-made Mustang.

Q. Name the type of Japanese torpedo bomber credited with sinking the U.S. aircraft carriers *Lexington, Yorktown* and *Hornet*.

A. The Nakajima B5N2, 144 of which participated in the Pearl Harbor attack. It was code-named Kate by the Allies.

Q. Name the site in Italy that was the target of the first U.S. air attack?

A. Naples harbor on December 4, 1942, bombed by U.S. B-24s.

Q. Who was New Zealand's top air ace?

A. Lieutenant Colonel Colin F. Gray, twenty-seven "kills."

Q. Where were the Luftwaffe headquarters in Paris located?

A. In the Luxembourg Palace on the Left Bank on Rue de Vaugirard.

Q. Who first used rockets in air combat in the Pacific?

A. The Flying Tigers, which became the U.S. Fourteenth Air Force.

Q. When did the U.S. Eighth Air Force make its combat debut?

A. In August 1942, from bases in England against targets in Germany.

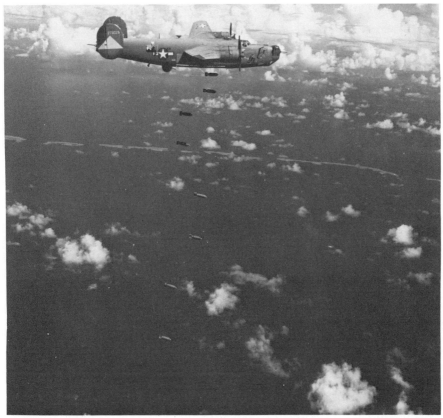

U.S. Air Force Photo

FACT: The American B-24 Liberator was used more extensively in the Mediterranean than in Germany because it had less armament and tended to catch fire when hit. In this photo, the famous Seventh Air Force in action over Truk atoll in the Pacific drops 500-pound bombs on Japanese positions. The name of the particular plane in this photo is the *Kansas Cyclone*.

Q. Identify the type of Japanese aircraft credited with sinking the British ships *Prince of Wales* and *Repulse* on December 10, 1941, in the Gulf of Siam.

A. The Mitsubishi G3Mi, code-named "Nell." A long-range medium bomber, it ended the war serving as a transport. Over 1,000 were built.

Q. What was the seagoing version of the RAF Spitfire known as?

A. The Seafire.

Q. How many tons of bombs did Britain drop on Germany?

A. Just over 645,920 tons.

Q. Where and when did the first B-29 Superfortress debut in a combat theater?

A. The first of the sixty-ton B-29s was sent to India in April 1944 and participated in its first raid on June 5, 1944 (the day Rome was liberated and one day before the Normandy invasion), on the railroad yards of Bangkok.

Q. Identify the first fighter designed for carrier use by the British?

A. The Fairey Fulmar. It was introduced to aircraft carrier service aboard the *Illustrious* in 1940 with the 806th Squadron.

Q. When did Boeing produce the last B-17 Flying Fortress for the U.S.?

A. April 9, 1945, at its Seattle, Washington, plant.

Q. Which Japanese aircraft, code-named Betty by the Allies but nicknamed Flying Lighter by U.S. pilots, brought the Japanese delegation to Ie-shima to negotiate the surrender?

A. The Mitsubishi G4M1 Navy medium bomber. It was the most widely produced of the Japanese medium bombers (2,446 were made).

Q. Identify the other British cities that the Luftwaffe raided during the same moonlight period of 1940 when they bombed Coventry.

A. Birmingham and Wolverhampton, along with Coventry, were Luftwaffe targets in November 1940.

Q. What position did Generalfeldmarschall Hugo Sperrle hold in August 1944?

A. Commander in Chief of the Luftwaffe, Western Front.

Q. When did the first U.S. heavy bombers begin operations against Germany from England?

A. August 1942.

Q. Identify the British fighter-bomber that was fast enough to intercept Germany's V-1 bombs.

A. The Hawker Tempest. It is credited with intercepting and destroying over 600 V-1 bombs.

Q. What was the name of the plane that President Roosevelt boarded in Miami on January 11, 1943, for the start of his trip to the Casablanca Conference?

A. The *Dixie Clipper*. When FDR boarded the plane, he became the first U.S. President to fly while in office. The pilot for the historic flight was Howard M. Cone, a Pan Am employee and Naval Reserve lieutenant.

Q. Which aircraft did Japan depend on to defend Tokyo during the last months of the war?

A. The Kawasaki Ki escort fighter–night fighter. The 10th Division depended on Nick, as the Allies called her, to repel the U.S. B-29s. Over 1,700 were produced.

Q. What was the last aircraft to leave Dunkirk?

A. A Westland Lysander with the name of *Lizzie*.

Q. Was the V-1 or V-2 known as the buzz bomb?

A. The V-1. Both were developed at Peenemunde.

Q. What was the maximum bomb load for a B-17, and what was the typical load for a mission over Germany?

A. Capable of carrying 17,600 pounds of bombs for short distances, the B-17 more frequently carried between 4,000 and 5,000 pounds on long-range raids.

Q. Which aircraft was the most used to train British pilots?

A. The De Havilland Tiger Moth.

Q. How did the Americans and British divide the bombing of Germany?

A. The British bombed at night and the Americans bombed during the day.

Q. Where did the U.S. launch the first air attack against the Japanese in the war?

A. In the Marshall and Gilbert islands on February 1, 1942, when a U.S. task force of two aircraft carriers and fifteen other ships initiated the largest U.S. offensive to date.

Q. Which aircraft was Japan's first low-wing monoplane fighter?

A. The Nakajima Ki-27, code-named Nate by the Allies. Introduced against the Russians in the Manchurian incident, it ceased to be manufactured in August 1940. However, the 3,400 planes in Japanese army flight groups saw considerable action through 1942.

Q. Whom did Churchill appoint as Minister of Aircraft Production?

A. Canadian entrepreneur Lord Beaverbrook.

Q. What other name was the German Junkers 87 more commonly known by?

A. The Stuka dive-bomber.

Q. What were the U.S. squadrons of the RAF called before they were reorganized under U.S. command on September 29, 1942?

A. The three U.S. units were the Eagle Squadrons.

Q. Identify the type of seaplane Japan produced in greater numbers than all others.

A. The Aichi E13A1, code-named Jake by the Allies. It was first used offensively on December 7, 1941, against the U.S. at Pearl Harbor. Catapulted from ships, its primary function was reconnaissance. Over 1,400 were produced.

FACT   The U.S. Navy ordered all ships to engage Axis ships discovered within twenty-five miles of the Western Hemisphere from April 18, 1941, on. The reasoning was that any ship so located could be considered hostile.

Q. How many bombing missions did Britain fly on all fronts during the war?

A. The RAF flew 687,462, dropping more than 1,103,900 tons of bombs.

Q. When did Germany launch the first V-1 bombs against London?

A. In June 1944, one week after the Allied landings at Normandy, France. They killed approximately 6,000 persons. (Hitler, bent on revenge against the English people, failed to use the V-1 against the critical military objectives of Southampton or Portsmouth, where the supply lines to France were being fed.)

Q. What was the name of the first U.S. jet plane flown during the war, and where did it fly?

A. The Bell XP-59 introduced U.S. aviation to the jet age on October 1, 1942, at Muroc in the Mojave Desert in California. The first U.S. jet fighter, the Lockheed P-80 Shooting Star, flew for the first time on January 8, 1944, but not in combat until June 1950 in Korea.

Q. Identify the type of Japanese aircraft responsible for downing ten U.S. B-29 Superfortresses on February 19, 1945.

A. The Nakajima Ki4411, produced in 1942. These high-altitude army interceptor-fighters were code-named Tojo by the Allies. Some 1,225 were produced.

Q. What were the aircraft losses of the British and Germans in the Battle of Britain?

A. The British lost 915 planes vs. 1,733 for the Germans.

Q. On what date did a German plane first drop a bomb on London?

A. August 25, 1940, in the financial center of London, the City. Previously the Luftwaffe bombed the docks and areas where war production was being carried out. There is evidence that the bomb was a stray hit, not intentional. The British retaliated by bombing Berlin.

Q. What type aircraft was the most produced by the U.S. in the war?

A. The Consolidated B-24 Liberator, which was used by the Army, Navy, RAF and other Allies. There were 18,188 of them produced.

U.S. Army Photo

Q. Who was the Deputy Supreme Commander at Supreme Headquarters Allied Expeditionary Force?

A. British Air Chief Marshal Sir Arthur Tedder, who is shown in photo above with the Supreme Commander, U.S. General Dwight D. Eisenhower, as the future U.S. President makes his VE-Day speech from Reims, France, in May 1945.

Q. Identify the RAF pilot who racked up the highest score during the Battle of Britain.

A. Sergeant Pilot Josef Frantisek, a Czech. He was one of many foreigners in the RAF, including Poles, Americans and others from the dominion. About 20 percent of the RAF was non-English.

Q. Where did the first Luftwaffe action in North Africa take place?

A. At Benghazi, on February 12, 1941.

Q. Which city suffered more damage from bombing, London or Berlin?

A. An area equal to ten times that destroyed in London was destroyed in Berlin by Allied bombings. Approximately 52,000 people, five times more than in London, were killed.

Q. Who originated the idea of a bombing raid on Tokyo that James Doolittle carried out?

A. Captain Francis S. Low, a submarine staff officer, submitted a plan for using Army bombers from aircraft carriers.

Q. Which country had the war's first jet engine bomber?

A. Germany, with the Arado Blitz, which went into service late in 1944.

Q. What enemy target marked the debut of the F6F Hellcat fighter on September 1, 1943?

A. Marcus Island, approximately 1,200 miles southeast of Tokyo.

Q. Who produced the only jet fighter aircraft flown in combat during the war?

A. Germany. The Messerschmitt Sturmvogel made its combat appearance by attacking a De Havilland Mosquito in July 1944. Approximately 360 Me-262 jets saw combat. (The world's first jet aircraft was a Campini N-1, which, piloted by Mario de Bernardi, connected Milan and Rome on August 28, 1940.)

FACT The B-29 Superfortress never flew on a mission against Germany. However, virtually all types of U.S. planes active in Europe saw action in the Pacific against Japan.

U.S. Air Force Photo

FACT: The Japanese had presented "Good Friendship" medals to various American citizens prior to the war. Lieutenant Colonel Jimmy Doolittle, in a ceremony just before his B-25s departed on their famous raid, attached several of the medals to bombs the planes would carry and drop on Japan. In photo above Doolittle attaches medal to the fin of a 500-pound bomb aboard the deck of the aircraft carrier *Hornet*.

Q. Which country produced the only rocket-propulsion fighter plane in the war?

A. Germany. The Messerschmitt Komet made its debut on July 28, 1944. About 350 of them were in service, and more were destroyed on landing than were shot down by the Allies. This is not to be confused with a jet aircraft.

Q. Identify the French rail center that was the first independent air-raid target of the U.S. Eighth Air Force.

A. Rouen on August 17, 1942. Until that time U.S. and RAF bombers had bombed jointly. The British did, however, provide Spitfire protection for the U.S. planes during the Rouen raid.

Q. What were Japanese aircraft losses in the 1941 attack on the Philippines?

A. Seven fighter planes. The U.S. losses were fifty-six fighters, eighteen B-17s and twenty-five other aircraft.

Q. What were Japanese vs. American air losses during the Okinawa campaign?

A. The Japanese lost over 7,800 aircraft, including a large number of kamikazes, as opposed to approximately 800 for the U.S.

Q. What was the last major Luftwaffe air raid during the war?

A. The January 1, 1945, raid on Allied air and naval bases in the Low Countries and France. Of 800 planes involved in the action, 364 were shot down, while the Allies lost 125 planes.

Q. What was the first target of a joint air raid by combined RAF and Russian aircraft?

A. A train on the outskirts of Dresden, Germany, on April 16, 1945.

Q. In which theater of war was the first helicopter rescue ever accomplished?

A. The China-Burma-India theater in April 1945, when U.S. Army Air Force Captain James L. Green was plucked out of the mountains. Green, who himself had been on a search-rescue mission for pilots, crashed in the mountainous jungle in Burma. Seriously injured, he was lifted to safety a week later by Lieutenant R. F. Murdock in a Sikorsky YR-4.

Q. Name the three Japanese sites that were targets for the last air raids of the war.

A. On August 14, 1945, five days after the second atomic bomb had been dropped, U.S. B-29s raided Akita, Isesaki and Kumagaya. The next day, August 15, all hostile actions ceased as VJ-Day was announced by the Allies.

Q. What was the main difference between the Japanese and German suicide plane pilots?

A. The Japanese kamikazes did not expect to return from a mission, while the German Sonderkommando Elbe pilots had the option to parachute to safety if appropriate. In all, Germany mustered approximately 300 volunteers (mostly from the Luftwaffe) for its suicide force. Their first action was against Allied bombers, which they crashed into in mid-air, on April 7, 1945.

Q. When Malta was bombed for the first time on June 11, 1940, was it German or Italian aircraft that were involved?

A. Italian. The British had only three old Gladiator biplanes with which to defend the island.

Q. When did the first German air raid on England take place?

A. On September 6, 1939, five days after Germany invaded Poland and two days after Great Britain declared war on Germany. The first air raid on London was January 12, 1940.

Q. When was Helsinki, Finland, bombed in the war for the first time?

A. November 30, 1939, by Russia.

Q. Who succeeded Goering as commander-in-chief of the Luftwaffe?

A. General Robert Ritter von Greim, after Goering's bold bid for power during the last days of the Third Reich. Greim committed suicide on May 24, 1945.

FACT The Japanese kamikaze pilots were responsible for sinking or damaging more than 300 U.S. Navy ships and causing approximately 15,000 casualties.

U.S. Army Photo

FACT: U.S. General Douglas MacArthur was an eighth cousin of British
Prime Minister Winston Churchill and a sixth cousin of U.S. President Franklin D. Roosevelt. All three wartime leaders had a common
ancestor, Sarah Barney Belcher of Taunton, Massachusetts. MacArthur is seen here (right) with General George C. Kenny, commanding
general of the Far Eastern Air Forces, aboard a transport bound for
Labuan Island, British North Borneo. As remarkable as the MacAr-
thur-Churchill-Roosevelt relationship was, consider this: At the outbreak of World War I, three of the most powerful European thrones
were occupied by first cousins: George V of England, Wilhelm II of
Germany and Nicholas II of Russia.

Q. When and how was the U.S. mainland bombed by a piloted aircraft during the war?

A. Catapulted from submarine I-25, a Lieutenant Fujita, flying a Yokosuka E14Y1, dropped four 167.5-pound phosphorus bombs along the timber coast of the State of Oregon in 1942. The Allied code name for the E14Y was Glen.

Q. Which nation is credited with employing the first major airborne operation, independent of other armed forces, in the war?

A. Germany, on May 20, 1941, when they attacked Crete.

Q. Which German city had the unfortunate distinction of being the "most bombed"?

A. Berlin.

Q. How long is Nagasaki, Japan, expected to have recordable amounts of radiation from the atomic bomb dropped there in 1945?

A. According to Dr. Shunzo Okashima of the Nagasaki Medical School, traces will remain for 24,360 years. However, at 540.7 pico curies per kilogram, he says it is not dangerous.

FACT: Germany launched more than 8,000 V-1 flying bombs against London starting on June 13, 1944. However, many were shot down by the R.A.F. over the English Channel. One that went amok after launching actually turned around and hit the Fuehrerbunker. About 2,425 managed to make it to targets in London. Starting on September 8, the first of 1,100 German V-2 rockets began to fall on England.

Naval Operations and Sea Battles

Q. What is considered the last classic battle between capital ships in the Atlantic ?

A. The battle between the German battle cruiser *Scharnhorst* and the British battleship *Duke of York* on December 26, 1943. The *Scharnhorst* was sunk after engaging British and Norwegian destroyers protecting a convoy en route to Murmansk. The *Duke of York,* three cruisers and six destroyers then finished the great ship off. Only thirty-six survived out of a crew of 1,900.

Q. Identify the U.S battleship that President Roosevelt, Admirals Leahy and King and Generals Marshall and Arnold were aboard when a U.S. destroyer fired a torpedo that exploded in its wake.

A. The *Iowa,* en route to the Teheran Conference, missed being hit when the *William D. Porter* discharged the torpedo by accident while performing a drill.

Q. Identify the British ship Winston Churchill was aboard when it was hit by two German torpedoes on October 30, 1939.

A. H.M.S. *Nelson.* He was in conference with several Royal Navy senior officers. However, both torpedoes failed to explode.

Q. From what aircraft carrier did James Doolittle launch his historic raid on Tokyo?

A. The *Hornet.*

Q. What was the significance of the flag raised on the Japanese carrier *Akagi* on Dec. 6, 1941?

A. It was the same flag that had flown on Admiral Heihachiro Togo's ship in the 1905 Japanese victory over the Russians.

Q. Who was the personal assistant to Admiral John Godfrey, director of naval intelligence in the British Admiralty?

A. Lieutenant Commander Ian Fleming, who years later would create James Bond.

Q. Identify the first German ship sunk in the war.

A. A submarine, U-39, sunk in the Atlantic by Royal Navy destroyers, on September 14, 1939.

Q. Identify the two famous British ships sunk in the Gulf of Siam on December 10, 1941.

A. The battleship *Prince of Wales* and battle cruiser *Repulse.* They had arrived at Singapore only eight days earlier as part of Britain's plan to exhibit its Far East strength. The Japanese lost three aircraft in the attack.

Q. Name the first Japanese ship sunk by the U.S. in the war.

A. The merchant ship *Atsutasan Maru,* on December 15, 1941, sunk by the U.S. submarine *Swordfish.*

Q. Identify the flagship of the Italian fleet in 1941.

A. The *Vittorio Veneto.*

Q. Identify the only Russian battleship sunk in the war.

A. The *Marat,* in September 1941.

Q. Where did the first Axis hostile action against Canadian territory take place?

A. At Vancouver Island in June 1942, when a Japanese submarine fired on a radio station there.

FACT A pair of German U-boats loaded with mines intended for placement in New York harbor were sunk by the Allies before they could complete their mission. However, the Germans did manage to mine ship lanes along the East Coast. The first ship lost from such mines was a merchant vessel, the *Robert C. Tuttle,* on June 15, 1942.

U.S. Navy Photo

Q. Who was the U.S. Navy's Commander-in-Chief, Pacific, on December 7, 1941?

A. Admiral Husband E. Kimmel. He had replaced Admiral James O. Richardson less than nine months earlier, on February 1. Though never formally charged with dereliction of duty or errors of judgment, he was humiliated and in some areas made the scapegoat for the disastrous attack on Pearl Harbor. Kimmel's book, *Admiral Kimmel's Story,* published thirteen years after the attack, details his fall from grace and subsequent battles to set the record straight.

Q. Identify the highest-ranking U.S. Navy officer killed in the war.

A. Rear Admiral Isaac C. Kidd, who died manning a machine gun aboard his flagship, the U.S.S. *Arizona,* on December 7, 1941. Every rank in the U.S. Navy is represented by the more than 1,100 men entombed in that ship.

Q. Who was Guenther Prien?

A. The German U-boat captain who attacked the British fleet at Scapa Flow in October 1939, sinking the *Royal Oak.* His skillful efforts made him a hero in Germany, while in Britain the episode greatly reduced morale.

Q. Identify the first British warship sunk in the war.

A. The fleet carrier H.M.S. *Courageous,* on September 17, 1939, off Ireland by a U-boat.

Q. Name the Japanese admiral who commanded the Pearl Harbor strike force?

A. Admiral Chuichi Nagumo.

Q. Identify the German officer who led the only naval action taken against the Allies on D-Day.

A. Lieutenant Commander Heinrich Hoffman, in the lead E-boat of a trio from the 5th Flotilla broke through a haze off the beaches at Normandy and confronted the invasion convoy. The three ships attacked with eighteen torpedoes and quickly retreated. One ship, the Norwegian destroyer *Svenner,* was sunk with thirty casualties.

Q. Which country had the largest navy and which had the smallest in the war?

A. The U.S. was by far the largest, with over 19,000 ships of all types. The total number of ships for all other nations was just over 5,500. New Zealand, with four ships, was the smallest.

FACT   The 2nd Battalion, 12th Regiment, of the U.S. Army's 4th Division used a tourist guide map of Paris that one of its officers traded two packs of cigarettes for in order to locate the unit's objective, the Prefecture of Police, during the liberation of Paris.

FACT: The idea of adding wooden stabilizers to the torpedo fins carried by Japanese aircraft so that the weapons would not hit the forty-five-foot bottom of Pearl Harbor was conceived by Commander Minoru Genda. It was the general opinion in U.S. Navy circles that the harbor was not deep enough for a torpedo-plane attack, as an approximately seventy-foot depth was considered minimal for success.

Q. Who was the first black to be commissioned in the U.S. Navy?

A. Ensign Bernard Robinson, in June 1942.

Q. Identify the first city to come under naval bombardment in the war.

A. Danzig. The German battleship *Schleswig-Holstein* attacked it approximately an hour after the dawn attack on Poland, September 1, 1939.

Q. Who was Commander C. H. Lightoller, R.N.R.?

A. One of the most distinguished participants in the Dunkirk rescue. He was the senior surviving officer of the *Titantic* and had been the major witness in the investigation of that disaster.

Q. Name the six Japanese aircraft carriers that launched planes against Pearl Harbor.

A. *Akagi, Kaga, Shokaku, Zuikaku, Horyu,* and *Soryu,* carrying a total of 423 combat planes.

Q. Name the Japanese naval officer who scouted the U.S. military operations at Pearl Harbor in October 1941.

A. Lieutenant Commander Suguru Suzuki, who was sent on the mission as a passenger aboard the *Taiyo Maru* out of Japan.

Q. Name the only Italian ship actually sunk twice during the war.

A. The cruiser *Gorizia,* which was scuttled and sunk off La Spezia on September 8, 1943, then salvaged, restored and sunk in June 1944 by the Allies. A similar fate awaited the German cruiser *Koenigsberg,* sunk in April 1940 and then again in September 1944.

Q. Identify the first major warship of any country sunk by aircraft bombing in the war.

A. The German cruiser *Koenigsberg* (8,350 tons) while docked in Bergen, Norway, was hit by two bombs from British Blackburn Skuas on April 10, 1940.

Q. Identify the U.S. ship sunk in the Atlantic on December 6, 1941, the day before hostilities began in the Pacific.

A. The merchant ship *Sagadahoc,* which was torpedoed by the Germans.

National Archives Photo

Q. Of the ninety-six warships in Pearl Harbor on December 7, 1941, how many were sunk or heavily damaged?

A. Eighteen. In addition to the warships the U.S. Navy had forty-nine other ships present, for a total of 145. An odd example is the U.S.S. *Chengho* (IX-52) which was a Chinese junk motor yacht that the Navy acquired on July 23, 1941, for use by the 14th Naval District (see Appendix for complete list of the 145 ships present). In photo above, the battleship *Oklahoma,* with its fourteen-inch guns and very little deck above water, is seen after the attack.

Q. Identify the city that was the target of the only action in which the German battleship *Tirpitz* had an opportunity to fire her mammoth guns.

A. Sister ship to the *Bismarck,* the *Tirpitz*'s only hostile firing of her eight fifteen-inch guns was against Spitzbergen, Norway, in September 1943.

Q. Who was responsible for creating the operational plans for the attack on Pearl Harbor?

A. Rear Admiral Ryunosuke Kusaka.

Q. Identify the first U.S. flagship captured in the Atlantic after war began in Europe.

A. The *City of Flint,* a cargo ship en route to Britain, was challenged and captured by the German pocket battleship *Deutschland.* The Germans contended that its cargo was war materiel.

Q. Identify the other ships involved in the famous battle between the *Hood* and the *Bismarck* on May 24, 1941.

A. The Royal Navy was represented in the engagement by *Hood* and the *Prince of Wales.* The Kriegsmarine's *Bismarck* was joined by the *Prinz Eugen.* These four giant ships fired at each other from 26,000 yards for about twenty minutes. *Hood* was sunk, and the *Bismarck,* which was hit and leaking oil, left a trail which led to her sinking within days.

Q. Identify the first U.S. ship attacked by enemy fire in 1941.

A. A German U-boat torpedoed the *Robin Moor,* a freighter, on May 21, 1941.

FACT By 1945 the pure Aryan composition of the Waffen SS was only a myth. Approximately 500,000 non-Germans filled the ranks of no less than twenty-seven of the forty Waffen SS divisions. This meant that over half of the service's strength was from other areas of Europe. In addition, there were Americans and Asians who served, but the largest numbers of non-Germans in the Waffen SS were Russian (nearly 100,000). Some of the countries represented included France (20,000); Holland (50,000); Norway (6,000); Denmark (6,000); Finland (20,000).

Q. Give the location and conditions of the sinking of the *Graf Spee*. When did it happen?

A. After fending off the three British cruisers *Exeter, Achilles* and *Ajax,* the *Graf Spee* made port in the neutral harbor of Montevideo, Uruguay. Rather than be captured upon leaving, the ship was scuttled by explosives in the River Plate. The date was December 17, 1939.

Q. Who was the captain of the *Graf Spee?*

A. Captain Hans Langsdorff, a veteran of the Battle of Jutland in World War I. Brokenhearted over the loss of his ship, he covered himself with a German Imperial Navy flag and shot himself on December 20, 1939, in Argentina.

Q. Identify the secret rendezvous base for the Japanese fleet preparing for the Pearl Harbor attack.

A. Tankan Bay in the Kuriles.

Q. Which area of Italy was the target of the amphibious invasion called Avalanche?

A. Salerno.

Q. Which U.S. Navy ship is credited with firing the first shot ever against a German ship?

A. The destroyer U.S.S. *Niblack,* on April 10, 1941, nearly eight months before the U.S. was officially in the war. The destroyer had just completed rescue operations involving the crew of a torpedoed Dutch ship. It dropped depth charges when it was believed the U-boat it had located was preparing to attack.

Q. What is considered the worst naval defeat experienced by the Allies during the war?

A. The Battle of the Java Sea, from February 27 through March 1, 1942, when the Japanese sank a total of ten U.S., British and Dutch ships.

Q. Name the first non-military U.S. ship sunk after the conflict began in 1939.

A. A U.S. merchant ship, the *City of Rayville,* made contact with a mine in the Bass Strait off Cape Otway, Australia, on November 8, 1940.

Q. Which naval battle is considered the greatest sea engagement of all time?

A. The Battle for Leyte Gulf. Japanese Vice Admiral Jisaburo Ozawa's fleet was sacrificed in an effort to lure away U.S. Admiral William Halsey.

Q. Identify the last ship to leave France in 1940 before the capitulation.

A. The Polish passenger liner *Batory,* which sailed for Britain on June 22 with the survivors of the Polish army who had fought in France. It departed from the port of St. Jean de Luz.

Q. Identify the first U.S. Navy ship hit by Japanese gunfire in 1941.

A. The gunboat *Tutuila,* which was on river duty near the Chinese capital of Chungking on July 30, 1941, more than four months before Pearl Harbor. The Japanese claimed the hit was unintentional but that the boat was too close to Chinese targets they were attacking. Japan apologized two days later.

Q. Name the first U.S. Navy ship sunk in 1941.

A. The U.S.S. *Reuben James,* escorting a convoy from Halifax, was sunk by the German submarine U-562 on October 31, 1941, thirty-eight days before Pearl Harbor. One hundred and fifteen lives were lost.

Q. Who sighted and reported the position of the *Bismarck?*

A. Early in 1941 the U.S. sent England some Catalina flying boats along with seventeen Navy pilots to train the British. Ensign Leonard B. "Tuck" Smith, the American co-pilot of Catalina Z-209, sighted the *Bismarck* on May 26 at 10:30 A.M. and radioed its location to the British fleet. The U.S. was officially neutral at the time.

Q. Why was the pocket battleship *Deutschland* renamed the *Lutzow?*

A. Because of Hitler's fear of the psychological effect if a ship named *Deutschland* was sunk by the enemy.

FACT   Civilian deaths in the war were more than double those of military personnel. In total, over 50 million people (civilian and military) died.

Q. Identify the Polish destroyer that participated in the Allied invasion of Normandy.

A. The *Poiron,* which was part of the convoy defense that escorted British and Canadian troops to their three beaches.

Q. Which battle holds the distinction of being the greatest aircraft carrier engagement of the war?

A. The Battle of the Philippine Sea. The Allied fleet had fifteen carriers against the Japanese fleet strength of nine. Overall fleet sizes were Allies 112 ships, Japan 55.

Q. Identify the first naval battle in which opposing ships never saw each other.

A. The Battle of the Coral Sea, May 3–8, 1942.

Q. Name the only U.S. battleship to get under way during the Japanese attack on Pearl Harbor.

A. The *Nevada,* which had already received a torpedo hit in her forward section. The oldest battleship in the Navy at the time, the *Nevada* later saw action at Normandy and Iwo Jima and was used as a target ship in the 1946 atom bomb tests off Bikini Island. She was sunk by the U.S. Navy during weapon tests in 1948.

Q. Who was PT boat commander Lieutenant John D. Buckley?

A. The U.S. Navy officer who on March 11, 1942, transported General Douglas MacArthur and Admiral F. W. Rockwell to Mindanao, where they took a B-17 to Australia.

Q. How was Admiral Yamamoto killed?

A. Acting on information received from Ultra code breakers, U.S. Navy P-38 planes shot him down after he took off from Rabaul on an inspection tour in April 1943.

FACT Carpet bombing was employed for the first time during the breakout at St. Lo after the Normandy landings. However, more than 100 troops of the 30th Division and Lieutenant General Lesley J. McNair, an observer, were killed when a portion of the 5,000 tons of explosives fell on U.S. troops by mistake.

Q. Identify the French admiral who became head of the Vichy government in February 1941.

A. Jean Louis Darlan. He was assassinated by a French monarchist in Algiers on December 24, 1942.

Q. Which naval battle is considered the U.S. Navy's worst defeat ever in a fair fight?

A. Savo Island, August 9, 1942. Despite fair odds, the U.S. Navy lost four heavy cruisers and one destroyer, 1,270 men killed and 709 others wounded. The Japanese lost thirty-five men and had another fifty-seven wounded. There was negligible damage to their ships in this battle that lasted thirty-two minutes.

Q. Identify the German military officer who first suggested to Hitler a cross-channel invasion of England.

A. Grand Admiral Erich Raeder, commander-in-chief of the German Navy, on May 21, 1940. Nearly two months later Hitler authorized the actual planning.

Q. Identify the high-ranking Philippine government official who escaped from the islands aboard the U.S. submarine *Swordfish* on February 21, 1942?

A. President Manuel Quezon.

Q. Which amphibious operation was the largest undertaken in the war?

A. The invasion of Sicily, with 1,375 ships directly involved, plus thirty-six more covering. Even the Normandy invasion exceeds it only if follow-up echelons are counted.

Q. In total, how many Allied convoys, including how many ships, were involved in the D-Day invasion at Normandy?

A. Fifty-nine convoys. U.S. Navy records say 5,000 ships; British records say 4,500.

Q. Identify the two largest battleships in the Japanese fleet at the outbreak of war.

A. The *Yamoto* and the *Musashi*. At 72,809 tons, they were the largest in the world.

Q. Name the French battleship the British sunk at Mers el-Kébir, near Oran, on July 3, 1940.

A. The *Bretagne.* In addition, the French lost two destroyers and the new battle cruiser *Dunkerque.* Over 1,300 French sailors died.

Q. Which branch of the U.S. military had the highest casualty rate?

A. The submarine command, with a rate of nearly 22 percent.

Q. What were the German one-man U-boats called?

A. *Biber,* or, in English, Beaver. They are credited with sinking at least a dozen merchant ships and nine naval vessels. The Allies sank seven of the twenty-nine-foot subs on one day, July 7, 1944.

Q. Identify Rear Admiral Kirk's flagship, which led the American task force on D-Day.

A. The heavy cruiser U.S.S. *Augusta,* which four months before Pearl Harbor transported President Roosevelt to Newfoundland to meet with Winston Churchill.

Q. Who commanded the Japanese carrier force in the Battle of the Coral Sea?

A. Vice Admiral Shigeyoshi Inouye.

Q. How many ships did the French scuttle at the Toulon navy base rather than let them fall into German hands?

A. Seventy ships.

Q. Identify the first U.S. submarine sunk in the war.

A. The *Sealion,* on December 10, 1941, at Cavite Naval Station in the Philippines while being overhauled. Badly damaged by the Japanese air raid, she was sunk by three U.S. Navy depth charges after being stripped of still useful equipment. The first U.S. submarine sunk while underway was the S-26 on January 24, 1942, off Panama.

FACT Major James Stewart, later colonel, flew twenty missions over Germany. In the postwar years he was promoted to general, attaining the highest rank of any member of the entertainment field who served in the war.

Q. Identify the British liner sunk by the Germans on the first day of the war in Europe.

A. The *Athenia,* with a loss of 112 lives, including twenty-eight Americans.

Q. Identify the task force that brought the first waves of troops to hit Omaha Beach.

A. Task Force O, Rear Admiral John L. Hall commanding.

Q. For which battle did Japan assemble its most powerful fleet in its history?

A. The Battle of Midway. It included eleven battleships and eight aircraft carriers. The total fleet consisted of more than a hundred ships.

Q. Which U.S. admiral was in command at the Battle of Midway?

A. Rear Admiral Frank Fletcher, who had to shift his flag to the cruiser *Astoria* after his flagship, the carrier *Yorktown,* had been badly damaged.

Q. Identify the U.S. river whose approaches were mined by the Germans.

A. The Mississippi, in July 1942. The mining was performed by a U-boat.

Q. How many submarines did the U.S. lose in the Pacific?

A. Forty-nine. The first was *Sealion,* three days after Pearl Harbor, the last was *Bullhead,* on August 6, 1945, the day the atom bomb was dropped on Hiroshima.

Q. Who replaced Admiral Erich Raeder as commander-in-chief of the German navy?

A. Admiral Karl Doenitz, on January 31, 1943.

FACT   The Japanese super battleship *Musashi,* 72,809 tons, 862 feet long (it was the same size as the *Yamato* but didn't have the feared eighteen-inch guns), was sunk in the battle of Leyte Gulf. The giant ship took twenty torpedo hits and seventeen bombs before going down along with half of her 2,200-man crew.

Q. Name the British destroyer responsible for capturing U-110 on May 10, 1941, the first submarine captured during the war.

A. H.M.S. *Bulldog,* under the command of Commander John Baker-Cresswell. This was not officially acknowledged until 1966 for security reasons. The British were able to get a German code machine (Enigma), cipher books, and other important information off the boat. However, the boat itself sank while being towed back to Scapa Flow.

Q. In total, how many naval battles were fought during the eight-month Guadalcanal campaign?

A. Six.

Q. Who were the two top Japanese officers in the Battle of Midway?

A. Admiral Isoroku Yamamoto was the overall commander, with Vice Admiral Chuichi Nagumo in charge of the carrier force.

Q. How many submarines did the U.S. lose in the Atlantic?

A. Three: S-26 on January 24, 1942; R-12 on June 12, 1943; and *Dorado* on October 12, 1943.

Q. What was the German Navy's U-boat strength when the war began?

A. There were forty-five battle-ready U-boats out of a total fleet of fifty-seven. Nine others were being built.

Q. What was the German U-boat strength during the Battle of the Atlantic?

A. Germany had 409 U-boats in operation in February 1943 and reached its peak in May that year, when there were 425 U-boats at large.

Q. Where and when did the British fleet score its first victory against the Axis in the war?

A. In mid-March 1941 in the Battle of Cape Matapan against the Italians in the Mediterranean.

Q. On the night of August 1–2, 1943, the Japanese destroyer *Amagiri* nearly changed the course of world history. How?

A. It knifed in two and sank PT-109 commanded by then Lieutenant John F. Kennedy.

U.S. Navy Photo

Q. Identify the U.S. admiral who ordered all ships to turn their lights on during the Great Marianas Turkey Shoot so returning pilots at night could locate aircraft carriers.

A. Vice Admiral Marc Mitscher, from his flagship *Lexington*. Eighty aircraft that had used up their fuel crashed in the water, but nearly all the pilots were rescued. A pensive Mitscher and the cap he made famous are seen aboard the *Lexington*.

Q. Identify the future Nixon cabinet member who was Lieutenant John F. Kennedy's commanding officer in the Solomon Islands.

A. Future Attorney General John Mitchell.

Q. What future U.S. Supreme Court Justice co-authored the official report on the loss of PT-109, commanded by then Lieutenant and future U.S. President John F. Kennedy?

A. While an intelligence officer for the flotilla that PT-109 was assigned to, Lieutenant Byron R. White co-authored the report. In 1962 Kennedy appointed him to the highest judicial bench in the land.

Q. What was the name of the U.S. ship on which the five Sullivan brothers perished?

A. U.S.S. *Juneau,* during the naval battle for Guadalcanal, November 12–15, 1942. It had been launched from the Federal Shipyard at Kearny, New Jersey.

Q. What ship did Prime Minister Winston Churchill arrive aboard for his meeting with President Roosevelt in August 1941 for the signing of the Atlantic Charter?

A. H.M.S. *Prince of Wales.*

Q. What was the historical significance of Japan's defeat at Midway?

A. It was her first ever naval defeat.

Q. Name the three U.S. submarines that sank the most enemy tonnage in the Pacific.

A. *Flasher* sank 100,231 tons, twenty-one ships; *Rasher,* 99,901 tons, eighteen ships; *Barb,* 96,628 tons, seventeen ships.

Q. Name the three most successful U.S. submarines in the Pacific based on the number of ships sunk.

A. *Tautog,* twenty-six ships for 72,606 tons; *Tang,* twenty-four ships for 93,824 tons; *Silversides,* twenty-three ships for 90,080 tons.

FACT   Three times as many bombs were dropped on Germany during the last eleven months of the war (after D-Day) than in all the years before.

Q. Who was Germany's most successful U-boat captain?

A. Lieutenant Commander Otto Kretschmer, credited with sinking forty-four Allied ships for a total of 266,629 tons. In addition, he sank one Allied destroyer. (Lieutenant Commander Guenther Prien, the most famous U-boat captain, sank twenty-eight ships for 160,939 tons, plus the British battleship *Royal Oak* at Scapa Flow.)

Q. What did the British change the name of the German submarine U-570 to after they captured it?

A. It went into the Royal Navy as the *Graph* after it was captured on its first combat patrol on August 27, 1941. It surfaced within range of RAF patrol planes, who depth-charged it, knocking out its lights and causing internal leaks. The crew panicked and forced the captain to surrender.

Q. Why are submarines called boats?

A. In the early development of the submarine as a combat weapon they were known as submersible torpedo boats.

Q. How much larger was the U.S. Navy at the end of the war than it had been on December 7, 1941?

A. It had twenty-one additional aircraft carriers, six more battleships, nearly 130 more submarines, seventy escort carriers and additional ships in every category.

Q. Name the only aircraft carrier in the German Navy at the outbreak of war.

A. The 23,200-ton *Graf Zeppelin,* which had been launched in 1938 but still wasn't commissioned. It could accommodate forty-two planes.

FACT   In the Battle of Leyte Gulf six of the seven ships in Japanese Admiral Nishimura's Southern Force C were sunk by Admiral Jesse B. Oldendorf's Seventh Fleet ships, which included five U.S. battleships that survived Pearl Harbor: *West Virginia, Tennessee, California, Maryland* and *Pennsylvania.* In a classic naval maneuver, Oldendorf's dreadnoughts formed a battle line at the entrance of Surigao Strait.

Q. Identify the British aircraft carrier whose Swordfish torpedo planes attacked the British cruiser *Sheffield* while tracking the German battleship *Bismarck.*

A. The fourteen Swordfish planes from the British aircraft carrier *Ark Royal* did it. However, all torpedoes missed.

Q. Name the five U.S. aircraft carriers and the six escort carriers lost in the war.

A. The five, alphabetically, were *Hornet, Lexington, Princeton, Wasp, Yorktown.* The six escort carriers were *Bismarck Sea, Block Island, Gambier Bay, Liscome Bay, Ommaney Bay,* and *St. Lo.*

Q. Identify the only U.S. aircraft carrier sunk in the Atlantic during the war.

A. The escort carrier *Block Island* was sunk by a U-boat on May 29, 1944, off the Azores.

Q. With regard to battleships and aircraft carriers, what were the strengths of the U.S. and Japan in December 1941?

A. The U.S. had nine battleships and three carriers in the Pacific fleet. Japan had ten battleships and ten carriers. Japan had more sea power in the Pacific than the combined Pacific fleets of the Americans, British and Dutch.

Q. Identify the only two battleships in the German Navy when the war began in 1939.

A. The *Gneisenau* and *Scharnhorst.* Three "pocket" battleships were also in the fleet: the *Deutschland, Graf Spee* and *Admiral Scheer.* (Though the *Bismarck* and *Tirpitz* had been launched in the spring of 1939, they were commissioned later. There were also two old battleships, the *Schlesien* and *Schleswig-Holstein* in reserve.)

Q. In what battle were the Royal Navy cruisers *Fiji* and *Gloucester* sunk?

A. The Battle of Crete. Two British battleships, the *Valiant* and *Warspite,* were hit also but survived.

Q. Identify the first U.S. ship struck by a Japanese kamikaze.

A. The escort carrier *Santee* during the Battle of Leyte Gulf. The first ship sunk as a result of a kamikaze was the escort carrier *St. Lo* in

the same battle. (Some escort carriers such as the *Santee* were
converted into aircraft carriers from tankers.)

Q. Where did the U.S. and Japanese meet for the first time in a major
naval action?

A. At the Battle of Makassar Strait on January 24, 1942. Four U.S.
destroyers attacked and sank four Japanese transport ships, causing heavy casualties.

Q. How successful was the U.S. submarine force in relation to its size?

A. Despite the fact that less than 2 percent of U.S. Navy personnel
were crew, back-up and staff attached to the submarine fleet, the
force is credited with 55 percent of Japan's maritime losses.

Q. Identify the German admiral who was killed at Christmas in 1943
when the battleship *Scharnhorst* was sunk.

A. Rear Admiral Erich Bey, along with nearly the entire ship's crew.

Q. What was the name of the Royal Navy submarine that is credited
with sinking the Italian troop transports *Oceania* and *Neptunia* in
September 1941?

A. The H.M.S. *Upholder.*

Q. Which amphibious assault was the largest in the Pacific war?

A. Okinawa. It was also the last amphibious assault.

Q. Under what circumstances was the U.S. aircraft carrier *Lexington*
sunk?

A. Badly damaged in the Battle of the Coral Sea, the *Lexington,* a
converted battle cruiser, was sunk by U.S. Navy fire rather than be
left to the marksmanship of the Japanese.

FACT The greatest damage to the U.S. Navy in the Pacific war was
not caused by the Japanese. A typhoon approximately 500 miles
off the east coast of the Philippines on December 17–18, 1944,
took a toll that included: 769 lives; damage to eight aircraft carriers; the capsizing of three destroyers; the loss of 150 planes
(off the carriers) and a number of other ships.

Q. Identify the four German fleet commanders during the war.

A. The four were Admiral Gunther Lutjens, who was lost when the *Bismarck* was sunk; Admiral Hermann Boehm and Admiral Wilhelm Marschall, both of whom were removed from command because of differences with Berlin; and Admiral Otto Schniewind.

Q. Where were the three aircraft carriers of the Pacific fleet during the attack on Pearl Harbor?

A. The *Saratoga* was en route to the U.S. for repairs; the *Lexington* was involved in delivering twenty-five scout bombers to Midway; the *Enterprise,* returning to Pearl after having delivered planes to Wake, sent eighteen planes ahead, which arrived during the Japanese attack.

Q. How did hostilities between Japan and the U.S. begin in the Philippines?

A. Twenty-two planes from the carrier *Ryujo* engaged the American seaplane tender *William B. Preston* in Davao Gulf, Mindanao, on December 7 (December 8, Manila time).

Q. Identify the flagship of the U.S. Pacific fleet on December 7, 1941.

A. The battleship *Pennsylvania,* which was in dry dock at the Navy Yard across from Ford Island and Battleship Row.

Q. How did the German battleship *Gneisenau* meet its end?

A. In February 1942 the *Gneisenau,* the *Prinz Eugen* and the *Scharnhorst* managed to slip away from the Norwegian coast. The *Gneisenau* was bombed by the RAF after it had made port in Germany and was rendered useless.

Q. Identify the first ship sunk at Pearl Harbor on December 7, 1941.

A. A Japanese midget submarine, sighted by a Catalina flying boat, was sunk by depth charges from the U.S. destroyer *Ward* at 6:45 A.M., more than an hour before the air attack. A second midget sub was sunk at 7:00 by another PBY.

Q. Besides her historic action at Pearl Harbor, why else is the date December 7 significant with regard to the U.S. destroyer *Ward?*

A. She was sunk at Ormac Bay in the Philippines on December 7, 1944, exactly three years after the "Day of Infamy."

U.S. Navy Photo

Q. Name the U.S. battleships moored at Battleship Row on December 7, 1941.

A. *Nevada, Arizona, Tennessee, West Virginia, Maryland, Oklahoma,* and *California.* The *Pennsylvania* was in Drydock One across the harbor. Only the *Arizona,* now a memorial, and the *Oklahoma* were totally lost. The others were repaired and saw action in the war. The photo above, taken by the Japanese, was made as the attack on Pearl Harbor began. Note the ripples in water from a bomb that missed its target.

Q. Identify the four Japanese aircraft carriers sunk or damaged at Midway.

A. Sunk: *Akagi, Kaga, Soryu.* Damaged: *Hiryu.*

Q. Who sighted the first submarine of the Japanese strike force near Pearl Harbor? Where? When?

A. At daybreak on December 6, Lieutenant James O. Cobb sighted and radioed ashore the presence of a submarine off Diamond Head. It submerged before an attack could be undertaken.

Q. Identify the German supply ship the British boarded in Norwegian waters to free nearly 300 British merchant navy personnel in February 1940.

A. The *Altmark,* which had been a tender to the pocket battleship *Graf Spee.* Though Norway protested this violation of her neutrality it wasn't a strong protest. The Norwegians had themselves conducted a search of sorts and had not discovered the British mariners, who were hidden below decks.

Q. When did the first official contact occur between the Japanese and Americans at Pearl Harbor?

A. At 3:42 A.M. on December 7 the mine sweeper *Condor*'s watch officer, Ensign R. C. McCloy, advised Quartermaster B. C. Uttrick that he had sighted a white wave about 100 yards to port of the ship. They identified it as the wake of a submarine periscope and contacted the destroyer *Ward.* However the sub escaped further detection.

Q. Who is credited with originating the concept of the kamikaze?

A. Vice Admiral Takijiro Ohnishi, who, during a senior staff meeting on October 19, 1944, first proffered the idea of planes with 550-pound bombs crashing onto American aircraft carriers.

FACT When the Germans invaded the U.S.S.R. their attack strength was three times as great as Napoleon's and included approximately 620,000 horse-drawn pieces of equipment and cavalry. The Germans also had 3,350 tanks. However, the Russians are believed to have had nearly 10,000 tanks. In all, Russia used more than 21,000 tanks in the war.

Navy Department Photo

Q. Identify the Japanese carrier-borne dive bombers that the Allies called
"Val" and which made up the first wave against the U.S. fleet at Pearl
Harbor.

A. Aichi D3A1. One hundred and twenty-six of them participated in the first
wave. The "Val" sank more enemy ships than any other dive bomber in
World War II. The one in the photo above was destroyed after it was
unsuccessful in pulling out of a dive.

Q. Identify the German passenger ship that was stalked by a U.S. Navy warship until the German captain elected to scuttle rather than be sunk or seized in 1939.

A. On December 19, 1939, while neutral, the U.S. cruiser *Tuscaloosa* followed and broadcast the position of the German liner *Columbus* in an effort to attract British warships. The U.S. ship had followed the *Columbus* since it left Mexico. The Germans scuttled off Cape May, New Jersey. No German protest was filed.

Q. What was the Japanese strength on Okinawa in April 1945?

A. Lieutenant General Mitsuru Ushijima had over 100,000 troops and 3,000 planes, many of which were the dreaded kamikazes.

Q. What was the name the German blockade-running ship *Odenwald* used while disguised as an American vessel?

A. *Willmoto.* The German ship was intercepted and captured by the U.S. destroyer *Somers* and cruiser *Omaha* in the Atlantic in early November 1941.

Q. Name the hospital ship in Pearl Harbor that the Japanese fliers recognized and did not attack.

A. The U.S.S. *Solace,* with its white hull and large red crosses was moored in East Lock.

Q. How and where was Japan's largest battleship, the 72,809-ton *Yamato* sunk?

A. On April 7, 1945, during the battle for Okinawa, the *Yamato* and an eight-ship screen boldly charged the U.S. fleet. She and five of the escort ships were sunk in less than two hours.

Q. Prior to December 7, 1941, when had so many U.S. battleships been together in port?

A. Not since the July 4 weekend that same year, also at Pearl Harbor.

FACT   There were 4,500 newspapers in Germany when the Nazis rose to power in 1933. By 1939, on the eve of war, the number was approximately 1,000, and they were controlled by or in sympathy with the Nazis.

Q. Who was commander-in-chief of the German Navy in 1939?

A. Admiral Erich Raeder, who hoped war would not begin before 1942, by which time he expected to have the navy at full combat strength.

Q. Identify the first Japanese ship captured by the U.S. in 1941.

A. A sampan sighted in the restricted waters at the mouth of Pearl Harbor at 6:48 A.M. on December 7, an hour before hostilities. The skipper of the sampan cut his engines and displayed a white flag when challenged by the destroyer *Ward*.

Q. Identify the Japanese admiral who led a squadron of kamikaze planes against U.S. ships at Okinawa.

A. Admiral Ugaki, with an eleven-plane group on August 15, 1945. He flew a Yokosuka D4Y2, code-named Judy by the Allies. Just over 2,000 of them were manufactured.

Q. What does CINCLANT stand for?

A. Commander-in-Chief Atlantic Fleet.

Q. What prompted Germany to issue the *Laconia* Order, which forbade U-boats from picking up survivors of ships?

A. The September 12, 1942, incident when an American aircraft attacked U-boats that had picked up over 1,100 survivors from the British transport *Laconia*. The ship had nearly 2,000 Italian POW's aboard when it was torpedoed and sunk. The Germans sent out a message for rescue assistance to ships of all flags, with assurances that they would not attack Allied ships that responded. Despite the flying of a giant Red Cross flag on one of the U-boats, the American attack was carried out. The Germans managed to pass the 1,100 survivors to the Allies, but the *Laconia* Order officially prevented any future operations of this scale between hostile nations on the high seas.

FACT   Even though hostilities between Britain and Germany had been a fact since early September 1939, Britain didn't restrict or confiscate German-bound shipments from England until November 21.

Q. Identify the first U.S. battleship launched after war began in Europe.

A. The U.S.S. *Washington,* on June 1, 1940. It was the first battleship added to the navy since the early 1920s.

Q. What was the Japanese hospital ship *Awa Maru* allegedly carrying when she was sunk by the U.S. submarine *Queenfish* on April 1, 1945?

A. According to an Associated Press story on May 3, 1979, the *Awa Maru* was sailing under a mercy-mission agreement with the Allies. However, over the years it has been suggested that the ship was actually transporting more than $5 billion in booty that the Japanese had collected during the war. Only one person of more than 2,000 aboard survived. (The *Awa Maru* had been many miles off the course the Allies agreed to for safe passage. Further, the *Queenfish* was not aware of the mission, the *Awa Maru* was hidden by fog and traveling at a speed equal to a warship's when the submarine fired four torpedoes. China began salvage operations in 1979 at the sinking site 190 feet below the surface in the Taiwan Strait. No mention was made of the treasure.)

Q. What was the name of the first U.S. Liberty Ship ever built?

A. The S.S. *Patrick Henry,* launched in September 1941. By the end of the war the U.S. produced and launched over 2,740, many in record time.

Q. Identify the two Japanese ships sunk in the December 11, 1941, invasion of Wake Island.

A. The destroyer *Hayate,* hit by shore batteries, and the destroyer *Kisaragi,* which was sunk by fire from U.S. Marine aircraft.

FACT The only U.S. aerial photographs taken of the Japanese attack on Pearl Harbor were made by Staff Sergeant Lee Embree aboard one of the twelve B-17 bombers that were arriving from California. Thinking the large aerial camera he swung out of a hatch was a gun, Japanese planes avoided the B-17.

U.S. Army Photo

Q. When was VE-Day?

A. May 8, 1945. The actual surrender was at 2:41 A.M. on May 7 in a school-house at Reims. However, the ceremony was repeated in Berlin, above, with Russian participation on May 8, which is the historical day the war in Europe ended. Seated center is Field Marshal Wilhelm Keitel with General Hans-Juergen Stumpff of the Luftwaffe to his right (left in photo) and Admiral Hans von Friedeburg of the Kriegsmarine. Picture was taken at Russian Headquarters in Berlin.

U.S. Army Photo

Q. When was VJ-Day?

A. August 15, 1945, is the day the war with Japan ended. However, the actual surrender was signed aboard the U.S. battleship *Missouri* in Tokyo Bay on September 2, 1945, and is celebrated as VJ-Day.

Q. How successful were the German Wolf Pack U-boat tactics off the U.S. Atlantic coast in early 1942?

A. Very. Eighty-seven ships were sunk during the first four months. After Allied ships only moved in convoy, the U-boats began activity in the Gulf of Mexico and sank forty-one ships in May alone.

Q. Name the Italian battleship sunk by German aircraft while en route from La Spezia to Malta on September 9, 1943.

A. The *Roma.* Italy had signed the armistice with the Allies the day before and was considered an enemy of the Reich.

Q. Which U.S. battleships sustained the least and which the greatest loss of life in the attack on Pearl Harbor?

A. Four crew members were killed aboard the *Maryland.* More than 1,100 were killed on the *Arizona.*

Q. Identify the two British battleships sunk at Alexandria by the Italians on December 19, 1942.

A. The *Queen Elizabeth* and the *Valiant.*

Q. Name the last major U.S. ship damaged in action in the war.

A. The battleship *Pennsylvania,* on August 12, 1945, two days before the war ended, was hit by a torpedo off Okinawa. The *Pennsylvania* was the only battleship present at Pearl Harbor on December 7, 1941, that was not seriously damaged.

Q. Name the ship the Japanese surrender was signed on.

A. The battleship *Missouri,* then Admiral Halsey's flagship.

Q. How was Admiral Sir Bertram Ramsay, Allied Expeditionary Force Naval Commander, killed?

A. In a plane crash in Paris on New Year's Day 1945.

FACT   The highest rate of casualties ever sustained by a United States Marine Corps regiment in one battle was 2,821 out of 3,512 in eighty-two days of the Okinawa campaign in 1945 by the 29th Marine Corps Regiment.

Q. What was the last naval surface engagement of World War II?

A. The action between the Japanese cruiser *Haguro* and a quintet of British destroyers in Malacca Strait. The *Haguro* was sunk there on May 17, 1945.

Q. Name the first U.S. aircraft carrier lost in the war.

A. Commissioned on March 30, 1922, and designated CV-1 (meaning she was the first U.S. aircraft carrier), the *Langley* was sunk near Java on February 27, 1942. She was at that time functioning as a seaplane tender. Hit by bombs from Japanese planes and badly damaged, she was ordered sunk by friendly fire.

Q. Identify the British aircraft carrier sunk by German U-boat U-81 near Gibraltar on November 15, 1941.

A. The *Ark Royal.*

Q. What was the aircraft carrier strength of Japan vs. the U.S. when hostilities began in 1941?

A. The Japanese had ten carriers, the U.S. had seven, of which only three were in the Pacific.

Q. Which aircraft carrier was the newest in the U.S. fleet when war was declared in December 1941?

A. The *Hornet.* Though completed prior to the outbreak of war, she had not yet made her maiden voyage.

Q. Identify the first U.S. Navy chaplain awarded the Congressional Medal of Honor.

A. Lieutenant Commander Joseph T. O'Callahan for his performance aboard the aircraft carrier *Franklin* after she was involved in a Japanese kamikaze attack off Japan in March 1945.

Q. Which nation suffered the greatest loss of life in a single ship sinking during the war?

FACT   The RAF marked the anniversary of Adolf Hitler's tenth year in power by conducting its first daylight raid on Berlin. The attack took place while the official ceremonies were under way.

A. Germany, when approximately 6,500 troops drowned during the evacuation of Danzig, April 16, 1945. A 5,320-ton merchant ship, the *Goya,* was hit by Allied torpedoes and because it was very much overweight sank almost instantly. This is the greatest single maritime loss in history, not only the war.

Q. Which country accomplished the largest mining of a seaway during the war?

A. The U.S. on January 25, 1945, when the coastal waters of Saigon, Penang and Singapore, among others, were filled with more than 360 mines dropped by B-29s.

Q. When did the first civilian merchant ship make a channel crossing between England and France since the last one in 1940?

A. In January 1945. After May 1940, only military ships, such as those involved in the raid on Dieppe and the Normandy invasion, had made the trip.

Q. Who was the British vice admiral who commanded a task force that became part of the U.S. Third Fleet in the Pacific, marking the first U.S.-British joint naval operations in that theater?

A. H. B. Rawlings, whose carrier task force linked up with U.S. naval forces on July 17, 1945.

Q. Name the last U.S. ship to be sunk by a Japanese kamikaze plane.

A. The destroyer *Callaghan,* off Okinawa on July 28, 1945.

Q. What became of the *Prinz Eugen,* Germany's only major fighting ship to survive the war?

A. Built in 1938, the *Prinz Eugen* served the Kriegsmarine with distinction. It survived bombing, torpedoing, striking a mine and the battle in which the *Bismarck* was sunk. She was turned over to the Allies at Copenhagen on May 9, 1945. She came to an inglorious end as a target ship during the United States atomic tests off Bikini Island in the Pacific in 1946. Another ship with a proud war record to participate in the Bikini tests was the U.S. battleship *Nevada,* present at Battleship Row in Pearl Harbor on December 7, 1941.

Historic Dates

Q. When, where and how did the United States sink the first German U-boat after entering the war?

A. Ensign William Tepuni, USNR, piloting a Lockheed-Hudson of Squadron VP-82, sank U-656 on March 1, 1942, off Cape Race, Newfoundland.

Q. When did the Japanese high command begin to plan the attack on Pearl Harbor?

A. In January 1941, more than ten months before it took place.

Q. When did U.S. and German warships first exchange gunfire in 1941?

A. September 4, 1941. The U.S.S. *Greer,* responding to a signal from a patrol plane, tracked U-652 for several hours. The patrol plane, British, dropped depth charges. The U-boat commander, Lieutenant Georg W. Fraatz, thought it was from the destroyer and fired two torpedoes. The *Greer*'s commander, Lieutenant Commander Frost, then attacked with depth charges. Neither side scored a hit. This was three months before the U.S. was officially at war.

Q. When did the Battle of Britain end?

A. October 31, 1940. It had begun on August 12.

Q. When did the Jews in the Warsaw ghetto offer the first armed resistance against the Germans?

A. January 18, 1943.

U.S. Air Force Photo

Q. When did Adolf Hitler commit suicide?

A. On April 30, 1945, in his bunker beneath the Chancellery in Berlin. In
photo above a tired-looking Lieutenant Harmon Smith, a U.S. navigator
who was shot down on a bombing mission over Germany on January 7,
1944, reads about Hitler's death in *Stars and Stripes* after having been
freed from a POW camp.

Q. Where and when did the U.S. sustain its first casualties in 1941?

A. In the torpedoing of the destroyer *Kearney* on October 17, 1941, by a U-boat off the coast of Iceland. Eleven U.S. Navy personnel were killed. Pearl Harbor was still several weeks away.

Q. When was Rome liberated?

A. June 5, 1944, one day before the Normandy invasion.

Q. When was the armistice between France and Germany?

A. June 20, 1940.

Q. When did the armistice between France and Germany actually take effect?

A. On June 25, 1940.

Q. When did the German naval war begin with Russia?

A. On June 15, 1941, German ships were ordered to conduct the "annihilation of Russian submarines without any trace, including their crews." This was seven days before Hitler's invasion of Russia and at a time when the two countries were still allied.

Q. What was the date of Rudolph Hess's flight from Germany?

A. May 10, 1941.

Q. Identify the first U.S. Navy vessel to sink a German U-boat, and when?

A. The destroyer *Roper* sank U-85 off Wimble Shoal near Hatteras in April 1942.

Q. When did Winston Churchill become First Lord of the Admiralty?

A. On September 3, 1939, the same day Britain declared war on Germany. Churchill had served as First Lord of the Admiralty for a time in World War I also, and news of his reappointment was signaled from ship to ship: "Winston is back."

FACT When Japan surrendered to the Allies in 1945 it still had over 2 million combat-ready troops and 9,000 aircraft. However, its navy had been all but eliminated.

Q. When did Winston Churchill become Prime Minister of Britain?

A. On May 10, 1940, upon the resignation of Neville Chamberlain. Churchill headed a coalition government made up of Conservative, Labour and Liberal ministers.

Q. When was James Doolittle's raid on Tokyo?

A. The morning of April 18, 1942, while an air-raid drill was in progress.

Q. When was Berlin bombed for the first time?

A. August 25, 1940, by the Royal Air Force. (The attack so shocked the Nazis that they cancelled a victory parade scheduled in Paris, fearing it would be too great a target for the RAF.)

Q. When did the heaviest and most severe Luftwaffe raid on London take place?

A. The night of May 10–11, 1941, when over 1,400 were killed and another 1,800 injured. Westminster Abbey and the House of Commons were among sites hit by bombs.

Q. When did the last air raid by the Western Allies on Berlin take place?

A. On Saturday, April 21, 1945, at 9:25 A.M. by the U.S. Eighth Air Force.

Q. When was the German battleship *Tirpitz* sunk?

A. November 12, 1944. The sister ship to the *Bismarck,* the *Tirpitz* was a constant target for the Royal Navy and RAF. The death blow came from five-ton bombs dropped by the RAF at Tromso Fjord. Over 900 sailors died when she capsized.

FACT　During the Battle of Midway a Japanese admiral and two aircraft carrier captains bound themselves to parts of their ships and went down with them rather than abandon the carriers. Captain Taijiro Aoki of the *Akagi* and Captain Tomeo Kaku of the *Hiryu,* along with Admiral Yamaguchi, who was aboard the *Hiryu,* made the ultimate sacrifice. Both of these carriers had participated in the Pearl Harbor attack.

Q. When did the U.S. Navy provide escort cover for a British convoy for the first time?

A. On September 17, 1941. The U.S. was to officially remain neutral for more than two months.

Q. What was the first major amphibious assault of the war in the Pacific? When?

A. Guadalcanal on August 7, 1942. Exactly eight months after the attack on Pearl Harbor, the 1st Marine Division invaded not only Guadalcanal but its sister islands of Tulagi, Gavutu and Florida.

Q. Why is September 15, 1940, known as Battle of Britain Day?

A. Because it marked the turning point in the proportion of Luftwaffe and RAF losses. The RAF lost twenty-six aircraft while downing sixty planes of the Luftwaffe.

Q. When and how was the U.S. aircraft carrier *Hornet* sunk?

A. On October 26, 1942, during the Battle of the Santa Cruz Islands north of Guadalcanal. Damaged by dive bombers, the *Hornet* was sunk by Japanese destroyers.

Q. When did the Allies invade Sicily?

A. July 10, 1943, in Operation Husky. It was captured on August 17.

Q. When did the 82nd Airborne Division make its combat debut?

A. In Operation Husky, the invasion of Sicily, July 1943.

Q. When did the 101st Airborne Division make its first combat jump?

A. D-Day, June 6, 1944.

FACT In November 1981 an American veterans group, the 6th Marine Division Association, announced plans to have Sugar Loaf on Okinawa dedicated as a memorial to the American and Japanese servicemen who fought in that historic World War II battle. Edward L. Fox, president of the Marine group, said it was seeking support from Japanese veterans. "Only in the event the Japanese are unable to participate will we undertake this as a strictly American project." (From a conversation with the author in December 1981.)

Q. When was the U.S.S. *Arizona* commissioned?

A. In 1916. The 608-foot dreadnought was the third U.S. Navy vessel to carry that name. In honor of the personnel who perished aboard her on December 7, 1941, no other U.S. Navy ships will ever carry that name. The earth-shattering explosion when the *Arizona* blew up occurred at 8 A.M., about fifteen minutes after the attack began. It is remembered by survivors as the most stunning single moment that day.

Q. When was the monastery at Monte Cassino bombed?

A. On February 15, 1944, 254 Allied planes bombed the historic site where St. Benedict is entombed.

Q. When did the Allies capture Cassino, Italy?

A. May 18, 1944.

Q. When did the B-29 Superfortress, made by Boeing, first bomb Japan?

A. On June 15, 1944. The first B-29 bombs fell on Toyko on November 24. The planes were used only in the Pacific.

Q. When was Saipan declared captured?

A. July 9, 1944. However, Japanese holdouts caused havoc for months after.

Q. What was the "darkest day" for U.S. submariners in the war?

A. October 24, 1944, when three subs, *Tang, Shark II,* and *Darter,* were all lost. *Tang* was hit by one of her own torpedoes that went amok off the coast of China; *Shark II* was sunk in Formosa Strait; *Darter* ran aground on a reef in Palawan Passage, bordering the South China Sea. This was the only day that the U.S. had lost more than one submarine.

Q. When did the Germans learn exactly how the Americans, British and Soviets would divide up Germany and occupy her?

A. In January 1945, five months before the end came. A copy of the secret plan had been captured from the British.

Q. When did Corregidor fall?

A. May 6, 1942.

FACT The United States Navy gathered what is considered by many to be the greatest exhibition of naval strength ever for the Japanese surrender ceremonies in Tokyo Bay in September 1945. The armada that made its way to the waters of the Japanese capital include twenty-three aircraft carriers, twelve battleships, twenty-six cruisers, and 313 destroyers and other ships, for a grand total of 374 vessels.

Q. When was Corregidor retaken by U.S. forces?

A. February 26, 1945. Nonetheless, there were over 50,000 Japanese who did not surrender until the end of the war.

Q. When was Vienna captured by the Red Army?

A. April 13, 1945.

Q. When did the German "blitz" on London begin?

A. The first bombs fell on the city on August 24, 1940.

Q. When did the Battle for Berlin begin?

A. At 4 A.M. on Monday, April 16, 1945, when the Russian artillery barrage began.

Q. When did the U.S. and RAF discontinue strategic bombing of Germany?

A. April 16, 1945, because few targets essential to the German war machine still existed.

Q. When did German troops in Italy surrender?

A. April 29, 1945.

Q. When and where was the first atom bomb tested?

A. At 5:30 A.M. on July 16, 1945, at Alamogordo Air Base, New Mexico.

Q. When did the Soviet Union declare war on Japan?

A. August 9, 1945, the day the U.S. dropped the second atomic bomb.

Q. When did the first Soviet troops actually penetrate the defenses around Berlin and reach the city?

A. Units of Marshal Koniev's armies entered the southern area of Berlin on April 22, 1945.

FACT　In a remarkable test of vessels of the same class going against each other, the U.S. submarine *Batfish* scored kills against three Japanese submarines in a four-day period off the Philippines in February 1945.

Q. Where and when did the Flying Tigers make their combat debut?

A. Over Kunming, China, on December 20, 1941.

Q. When did the Italians overthrow Mussolini?

A. On July 25, 1943, the Fascist Grand Council voted nineteen to seven to put command of Italy's armed forces under King Victor Emmanuel III.

Q. When did Italy sign the armistice with the Allies?

A. September 8, 1943. From that time on Italian troops vigorously fought against Germany.

Q. When did Italy officially announce that it was out of the war as a member of the Axis?

A. At 8 P.M. in the evening of September 8, 1943.

Q. When was the Nazi flag raised on Mount Elbrus, the highest peak in the Caucasus Mountains.

A. August 21, 1942.

Q. When was the U.S. Eighth Air Force created?

A. January 28, 1942, under the command of General Carl Spaatz.

Q. When did the U.S. declare war on Germany and Italy?

A. The Germans, followed quickly by the Italians, declared war on the U.S. on December 11, 1941. The U.S. Congress responded with its own war vote that same afternoon.

Q. When were the Germans halted and reversed in their campaign against Russia?

A. On December 5, 1941, when certain panzer units were within twenty-five miles of Moscow. The Russians mounted a counteroffensive on December 6 and began their push that would not end until forty-one months later, in Berlin.

FACT The U.S. Navy trained naval personnel from fourteen different countries at its Submarine Chaser Training Center in Miami, Florida, during 1942–43.

Q. When did the Luftwaffe bomb Moscow?

A. July 21, 1941, one day short of a full month after war between the two former allies was declared.

Q. When did the Soviet Air Force first bomb Berlin?

A. August 8, 1941, using Ilyushin IL-4 medium bombers.

Q. When was Crete invaded by the Germans?

A. On May 20, 1941. It marked the first time that paratroopers and gliders constituted the main body of an attack force. Over 22,700 German airborne troops participated.

Q. What was the date of the Soviet-German non-aggression pact?

A. August 23, 1939.

Q. On what date did the invading German troops reach the sea at Abbeville, France?

A. On May 21, 1940, eleven days after they had crossed the Belgian and Dutch frontiers, thus ending the "phony war" that had existed since September 1939.

Q. When did General Charles de Gaulle announce the formation of the Free French government?

A. On October 27, 1940. The power of the government was to be in the care of the general and his defense council.

Q. When did the RAF execute its first air raid on Italy?

A. The night of June 11–12, 1940. Ten planes bombed the Fiat plant at Turin and the surrounding area; two bombed Genoa.

Q. When did the invasions of Denmark and Norway begin?

A. April 9, 1940. Denmark surrendered the same day.

FACT   All during the war U.S. forces in other services envied the legendary meals enjoyed by the Navy. However, many simply would not believe that the U.S. Navy actually had a ship whose sole purpose was to make ice cream for sailors in the South Pacific, yet it was true. The ship was capable of producing over 5,000 gallons of ice cream per hour.

Q. When did RAF planes first enter air space over Berlin?

A. During the night of October 1–2, 1939, on a propaganda leaflet-dropping mission.

Q. When did Warsaw surrender to Germany?

A. September 27, 1939, less than four weeks after the war began.

Q. When did the Russians begin to occupy Poland?

A. September 17, 1939.

Q. On what date did France enter the war?

A. September 3, 1939.

Q. When did Ireland announce its neutrality?

A. On September 2, 1939, the day after the German attack on Poland and the day before Britain, France, Australia, New Zealand and India declared war on Germany.

Q. When did Lithuania, Latvia and Estonia fall to the Soviets?

A. In June 1940.

Q. When was Paris declared an open city?

A. On June 13, 1940.

Q. When did Singapore surrender?

A. February 15, 1942.

Q. Where and when did the first saturation bombing raid take place?

A. May 30, 1942, by 1,000 RAF planes on the German city of Cologne.

Q. When were the first Grumman F6F Hellcats used in combat?

A. On August 31, 1943, from the carrier *Yorktown* for the battle of Marcus Island in the Pacific.

FACT In a remarkable display of precision bombing on October 31, 1944, RAF planes bombed the Gestapo headquarters at Aarhus, Denmark, without damaging two hospitals that were hardly 100 yards away.

U.S. Army Photo

Q. Name the twelve Allied and Japanese signers of the instrument of surrender aboard the *Missouri*.

A. The ten Allied signers were General Douglas MacArthur, for the Allied
powers; Admiral Chester Nimitz for the U.S.; General Hsu Yung-chang,
for China; Admiral Sir Bruce Fraser, for the U.K.; General K. Derev-
yanko, for the Soviet Union; General Sir Thomas Blamey, for Australia;
Colonel Moore Gosgrove, for Canada; General Jacques Leclerc, for France;
Admiral C. Helfrich, for the Netherlands; and Air Vice Marshal Sir L. M.
Isitt, for New Zealand. The two Japanese signers were Foreign Minister
Mamoru Shigemitsu, on behalf of the Emperor of Japan, and General Yo-
shijiro Umezu, for the Imperial General Headquarters. This formal sign-
ing officially ended 1,364 days, five hours and fourteen minutes of World
War II in the Pacific. The exact time of signing was 9:04 A.M.

Q. When did the invasion of Salerno, Italy, begin?

A. At 3:30 A.M. on September 9, 1943, by the U.S. Fifth Army under General Mark Clark.

Q. When did the Allies invade Anzio and Nettuno, Italy?

A. January 22, 1944.

Q. When did CINCPAC issue the order to "Cease all offensive operations against Japan"?

A. August 15, 1945. However all ships maintained full defensive alert until the formal surrender was signed on September 2.

Q. When did General Douglas MacArthur fulfill his pledge and return to the Philippines?

A. October 20, 1944, at Palo, Leyte. He returned 948 days after having been ordered to leave by President Franklin Roosevelt.

Q. What was the date the atomic bomb was dropped on Hiroshima?

A. August 6, 1945, by a B-29 named *Enola Gay*. The pilot was Colonel Paul W. Tibbets, the co-pilot was Captain Robert Lewis, the plane's actual commander.

U.S. Marine Corps Photo

Q. When did the U.S. amphibious landings on Okinawa begin?

A. At 8:30 A.M., April 1, 1945, Easter Sunday. The battle lasted eighty-two days. In the photo above, Marine Corporal Fenwick H. Dunn gives the candy from his K rations to an aged woman on Okinawa.

FACT: More than 7.5 million Europeans were pressed into forced labor for the Third Reich when calls for volunteers fell short of manpower needs. In addition, approximately 2 million prisoners of war were also forced to work in the Nazi war machine. The poster shown here was used in early years to recruit French workers by suggesting that helping the Nazis would save Europe from the Russians.

Appendix

The Fastest Fighter Planes of the War

There were sixty-four different versions of fighter planes, land-based and carrier-borne, produced by Allied and Axis powers during the war. In addition, there were fighter-bombers. Below are the nineteen fastest fighters that had maximum speeds over 400 miles per hour.

Plane/Country	Maximum Speed	Maximum Range
Messerschmitt Me-263, Germany	596 mph (rocket)	N.A.
Messerschmitt Me-262, Germany	560 mph (jet)	650 miles
Heinkel He-162A, Germany	553 mph	606 miles
P-51-H, United States	487 mph	850 miles
Lavochkin La-11, Russia	460 mph	466 miles
Spitfire XIV, Great Britain	448 mph	460 miles
Yakovlev Yak-3, Russia	447 mph	506 miles
P-51-D Mustang, United States	440 mph	2,300 miles
Tempest VI, Great Britain	438 mph	740 miles
Focke-Wulf FW-190D, Germany	435 mph	560 miles
Lavochkin 9, Russia	429 mph	1,078 miles
P-47-D Thunderbolt, United States	428 mph	1,000 miles
Lavochkin La-7, Russia	423 mph	392 miles
F4U Corsair, United States	417 mph	1,015 miles
Yakovlev Yak-9P, Russia	416 mph	889 miles
P-38-L Lightning, United States	414 mph	460 miles
Typhoon, Great Britain	412 mph	510 miles
Lavochkin La-5FN, Russia	401 mph	528 miles
Messerschmitt Me-109G, Germany	400 mph	460 miles

U.S. Ships Present at Pearl Harbor, December 7, 1941

Although most references agree that there were ninety-six *warships* in Pearl Harbor during the Japanese attack and that eighteen of them were sunk, it is rarely mentioned that the U.S. Navy and Coast Guard had forty-nine *other* ships there at the time. The complete list of 145 ships includes:

Allen (DD-66)
Antares (AKS-3)
Argonne (AG-31)
Arizona (BB-39)
Ash (YN-2)
Avocet (AVP-4)
Aylwin (DD-355)
Bagley (DD-386)
Blue (DD-387)
Bobolink (AM-20)
Breese (DM-18)
Cachalot (SS-170)
California (BB-44)
Case (DD-370)
Cassin (DD-372)
Castor (AKS-1)
CG-8 (USCG)
Chengho (IX-52)
Chew (DD-106)
Cinchona (YN-7)
Cockatoo (AMc-8)
Cockenoe (YN-47)
Condor (AMc-14)
Conyngham (DD-371)
Crossbill (AMc-9)
Cummings (DD-365)
Curtiss (AV-4)
Dale (DD-353)
Detroit (CL-8)
Dewey (DD-349)
Dobbin (AD-3)
Dolphin (SS-169)
Downes (DD-375)
Farragut (DD-348)
Gamble (DM-15)
Grebe (AM-43)
Helena (CL-50)
Helm (DD-388)
Henley (DD-391)
Hoga (YT-146)
Honolulu (CL-48)

Hulbert (AVD-6)
Hull (DD-350)
Jarvis (DD-393)
Keosangua (AT-38)
MacDonough (DD-351)
Manuwai (YFB-17)
Marin (YN-53)
Maryland (BB-46)
Medusa (AR-1)
Monaghan (DD-354)
Montgomery (DM-17)
Mugford (DD-389)
Narwhal (SS-167)
Navajo (AT-64)
Neosho (AO-23)
Nevada (BB-36)
New Orleans (CA-32)
Nokomis (YT-142)
Oglala (CM-4)
Oklahoma (BB-37)
Ontario (AT-13)
Osceola (YT-129)
Patterson (DD-392)
Pelias (AS-14)
Pennsylvania (BB-38)
Perry (DMS-17)
Phelps (DD-360)
Phoenix (CL-46)*
Preble (DM-20)
Pruitt (DM-22)
PT-20
PT-21
PT-22
PT-23
PT-24
PT-25
PT-26
PT-27
PT-28
PT-29
PT-30

PT-42
Pyro (AE-1)
Rail (AM-26)
Raleigh (CL-7)
Ralph Talbot (DD-390)
Ramapo (AO-12)
Ramsay (DM-16)
Reedbird (AMc-30)
Reid (DD-369)
Reliance (USCG)
Rigel (AR-11)
Sacramento (PG-19)
St. Louis (CL-49)
San Francisco (CA-38)
Schley (DD-103)
Selfridge (DD-357)
Shaw (DD-373)
Sicard (DM-21)
Solace (AH-5)
Sotoyomo (YT-9)
Sumner (AG-32)
Sunnadin (AT-28)
Swan (AVP-7)
Taney (PG-37) (USCG)†
Tangier (AV-8)
Tautog (SS-199)
Tennessee (BB-43)
Tern (AM-31)
Thornton (AVD-11)
Tiger (PC-152) (USCG)
Tracy (DM-19)
Trever (DMS-16)
Tucker (DD-374)
Turkey (AM-13)
Utah (AG-16)
Vega (AK-17)
Vestal (AR-4)
Vireo (AM-52)
Wapello (YN-56)
Ward (DD-139)
Wasmuth (DMS-15)

West Virginia (BB-48)	YNg-17	YT-152
Whitney (AD-4)	YO-21	YT-153
Widgeon (ASR-1)	YO-43	YW-16
Worden (DD-352)	YP-108	*Zane* (DMS-14)
YG-15	YP-109	YO-30
YG-17	YTT-3	YO-44
YG-21	YT-119	
YMT-5	YT-130	

* The *Phoenix* (CL-46) was sold to Argentina in 1951 and renamed *General Belgrano.* On May 2, 1982, the cruiser was sunk off the Falkland Islands by a British submarine during the hostilities between the two countries over sovereignity of the Falklands. It was the first sinking of a ship by a submarine since the end of World War II.

† The *Taney,* a 327-foot-long endurance cutter, remained in U.S. service longer than any of the above-mentioned vessels. Still on active service on December 7, 1981, forty years after the attack, the *Taney* participated in memorial services at Pearl Harbor.

Whatever Happened to the *Enola Gay?*

Donated to the Smithsonian Institution by the Department of Defense, the B-29 that dropped the first atom bomb on a Japanese city was, in 1981, lying in parts in a hangar in Silver Spring, Maryland.

"I'd like to see it donated to New Jersey and have it displayed at Teterboro Airport. It was my plane and I lived in that state all my life," noted Captain Robert Lewis, the ship's commander. Lewis was obliged to take part in the Hiroshima mission as co-pilot in his own plane when the 509th Composite Group's commander Colonel Paul Tibbets elected to participate in the flight.

When asked about the naming of the plane, Lewis replied, "The naming of the plane was reserved for the ship's commanding officer, and that was me. I would have named it *Pearl Harbor* or *Indianapolis* after the U.S. Navy cruiser that delivered the uranium to Tinian Island and was then sunk by a Japanese sub. That was the greatest single naval loss we ever suffered at sea." Tibbets named the plane after his mother.

"That B-29, my B-29, came off the assembly line in Omaha, Nebraska, on June 16, 1945, and was christened by a young lady named Dorothy Norgood," Lewis added. He said this last bit of information is not common knowledge. "I'm sure Tibbets doesn't even know that!" (from a personal conversation with the author on December 12, 1981.)

The 22 Largest Battleships in World War II

Until the Japanese attack on Pearl Harbor the navies of the world considered battleships the ultimate sea weapon; and the larger and heavier they were was supposed to indicate something about a country's sea power. Ironically, the Japanese launched the two largest battleships ever built. But her aircraft carriers were the weapon she depended on for the initiation of hostilities with the U.S., and it was U.S. aircraft carriers that turned the tide of war in the Pacific. It is interesting to note that while Japan's *Yamato*-class battleships were by far the heaviest, the United States' *Iowa*-class dreadnoughts were the longest.

Ship/Country	Tons	Length
Yamato, Japan	72,809	862
Musashi, Japan	72,809	862
Iowa, United States	55,710	887
New Jersey, United States	55,710	887
Missouri, United States	55,710	887
Wisconsin, United States	55,710	887
Bismarck, Germany	50,153	823
Tirpitz, Germany	50,153	823
Richelieu, France	47,500	812
Jean Bart, France	47,500	812
Hood, Great Britain	46,200	860
North Carolina, United States	44,800	729
Washington, United States	44,800	729
King George V, Great Britain	44,780	754
Prince of Wales, Great Britain	44,780	754
Duke of York, Great Britain	44,780	754
Anson, Great Britain	44,780	754
Howe, Great Britain	44,780	754
Nagato, Japan	42,785	725
Mutsu, Japan	42,785	725
Tennessee, United States	40,500	624
California, United States	40,500	624

The U.S.S. *Arizona*

Compared to these 40,000-plus giants, the most famous U.S. battleship was small. The third American ship to carry the name *Arizona* was placed in commission in 1916 and had a normal displacement of 31,400 tons and was 608 feet long. Of the approximately 1,550 Navy and Marine Corps personnel aboard her on December 7, 1941, only 289 survived. A campaign to raise $500,000 for a memorial was begun in 1957 and included a benefit performance by entertainer Elvis Presley as well as support from the popular television show *This Is Your Life* and from newspapers across the country. The memorial, dedicated on Memorial Day 1962, spans the *Arizona*, which was never raised from its watery grave.

U.S. Army Photo

Did Eva Braun and Hitler's Daughter Escape?

The November 1981 issue of the British Medical Association's *News Review* published the findings of a ten-year study on the World War II records of Adolf Hitler and his mistress Eva Braun, including dental evidence by a California research team that cast doubt on her death. According to the report, Hitler's dental records matched those of one of the thirteen bodies found near the bunker in Berlin on twenty-six points, including a unique window crown. The report said the odontological data for the female body presumed to be Eva Braun's did not agree with her personal records. The report stated further that if Eva Braun died in the bunker she may be buried elsewhere. It also pointed to the possibility that she may have escaped. A German U-boat, U-977, was the last German ship to surrender on August 17, 1945—more than three months after the war had ended. It surrendered in Argentina. It immediately became suspect of having transported Hitler or other ranking Nazis out of Germany. The controversy as to why this U-boat remained at large for so long after the end of hostilities has never been settled, according to doubters and those who believe it carried Eva Braun and others to freedom. In the accompanying photo, Hitler and Eva are shown with a child, Uschi, who was thought to have been Hitler's daughter.

The 20 Leading U-Boat Commanders of
the German Kriegsmarine*

As with fighter pilots, the U-boat commanders dominated their area of warfare. It is interesting to note that the United States' top submarine commander, Richard O'Kane, would place seventh in the German top twenty U-boat commanders based on the number of ships sunk.

Commander/U-Boat	Ships Sunk	Number of Patrols
Otto Kretschmer, U-23 and U-99	45	16
Wolfgang Luth, U-9, U-138, U-43, U-181	44	14
Joachim Schepko, U-3, U-19, U-100	39	14
Erich Topp, U-57, U-552	35	13
Victor Schutze, U-25, U-103	34	7
Heinrich Liebe, U-38	30	9
Karl F. Merten, U-68	29	5
Guenther Prien, U-47	29	10
Joh. Mohr, U-124	29	6
Georg Lassen, U-160	28	4
Carl Emmermann, U-172	27	5
Herbert Schultze, U-48	26	8
Werner Henke, U-515	26	6
Heinrich Bleichrodt, U-48, U-109	25	8
Robert Gysae, U-98, U-177	25	8
Klaus Scholtz, U-108	24	8
Reinhard Hardegen, U-147, U-123	23	1
H. Lehmann-Willenbroch, U-5, U-96, U-256	22	10
Engelbert Endrass, U-46, U-567	22	9
Ernst Kals, U-130	19	5

*Based on number of ships sunk. Gross tons considered only for ranking when number of ships is equal. Other commanders who sank nineteen ships are not included if total tonnage was below 138,500.

FACT   Several towns in Florida refused to respond to blackout precautions in early 1942 when German U-boats were enjoying what they called the American Hunting Season and the Happy Time. During this period U-boats were sinking ships silhouetted against the U.S. coast. In one two-week period U-boats sank twenty-five ships. Towns were reluctant to turn off their lights, as it would have an adverse effect on the tourist trade.

U.S. Navy Photo

Q. How many Japanese submarines were in the Advance Expeditionary Force that attacked Pearl Harbor?

A. Twenty-seven, five of which carried midget two-man submarines. This one is shown on display at Bellows Field, Oahu, Hawaii. The midgets made long voyages "piggy-back" on larger subs and were set loose as they neared their target.

The 20 Leading Submarine Commanders of the United States Navy*

Commander/Submarine	Ships Sunk	Number of Patrols
Richard H. O'Kane, *Tang*	31	5
Eugene B. Fluckey, *Barb*	25	5
Slade D. Cutter, *Seahorse*	21	4
Samuel D. Dealey, *Harder*	20½	6
William S. Post, Jr., *Gudgeon* and *Spot*	19	7
Reuben T. Whitaker, S-44 and *Flasher*	18½	5
Walter T. Griffith, *Bowfin* and *Bullhead*	17	5
Dudley W. Morton, R-5 and *Wahoo*	17	6
John E. Lee, S-12, *Grayling* and *Croaker*	16	10
William B. Sieglaff, *Tautog* and *Tench*	15	7
Edward E. Shelby, *Sunfish*	14	5
Norvell G. Ward, *Guardfish*	14	5
Gordon W. Underwood, *Spadefish*	14	3
John S. Coye, Jr., *Silversides*	14	6
Glynn R. Donaho, *Flying Fish* and *Picuda*	14	7
George E. Porter, Jr., *Bluefish* and *Sennet*	14	6
Henry G. Munson, S-38, *Crevalle* and *Rasher*	13	9
Robert E. Dornin, *Trigger*	13	3
Charles O. Triebel, S-15 and *Snook*	13	8
Royce L. Gross, *Seawolf* and *Boarfish*	13½	7

*Based on number of ships sunk. Gross tons sunk considered only for ranking when number of ships is equal. Other commanders who sank thirteen ships are not included if total tonnage was below 80,000.

The Leading Fighter Pilots, All Nations

To earn the distinction of being an ace a pilot had to score a minimum of five "kills," or victories. As difficult as that was, the list of all the aces would fill several pages (there were 330 in the U.S. Navy alone). Those listed here are aces who earned the title *five times over or more*, meaning a minimum of twenty-five "kills." In addition, thirty-eight German fighter Aces *scored over 100 "kills,"* making them the unchallenged super aces of the war. In the interest of brevity, only German super aces with more than 250 kills each have been listed.

Fighter Ace/Nationality	*Number of Kills*
Erich Hartmann, Germany	352
Gerhard Barkhorn, Germany	301
Gunther Rall, Germany	275
Otto Kittel, Germany	267
Walther Nowotny, Germany	255
Hiroyishi Nishizawa, Japan	87*
Shoichi Sugita, Japan	80*
Hans H. Wind, Finland	75
Saburo Sakai, Japan	64†
Ivan Kozhedub, Russia	62
Aleksandr Pokryshkin, Russia	59
Grigorii Rechkalov, Russia	58
Hiromichi Shinohara, Japan	58
Nikolai Gulaev, Russia	57
Waturo Nakamichi, Japan	55
Takeo Okumura, Japan	54
Naoshi Kanno, Japan	52
Kirill Yevstigneev, Russia	52
Satoshi Anabuki, Japan	51
Yasuhiko Kuroe, Japan	51
Dimitrii Glinka, Russia	50
Aleksandr Klubov, Russia	50
Ivan Pilipenko, Russia	48
Arsenii Vorozheikin, Russia	46
Vasilii Kubarev, Russia	46
Nikolai Skomorokhov, Russia	46
J. Pattle, South Africa	41
Richard I. Bong, U.S.A.	40
Thomas B. McGuire, U.S.A.	38
J. E. Johnson, Great Britain	38
A. G. Malan, South Africa	35
David McCampbell, U.S.A.	34
P. H. Closterman, France	33
B. Finucane, Ireland	32

*Some works credit Shoichi Sugita with 120 kills and Nishizawa with 103.

†Saburo Sakai has been credited with 80 kills in another work. (Though this author is satisfied that the figures given here are correct, the discrepancies have been pointed out because they do exist.)

Fighter Ace/Nationality	Number of Kills
G. F. Beurling, Canada	31⅓
Frances S. Gabreski, U.S.A.	31
J. R. D. Graham, Great Britain	29
R. R. S. Tuck, Great Britain	29
C. R. Caldwell, Australia	28½
Gregory Boyington, U.S.A.	28
J. Frantisek, Czechoslovakia	28
Robert S. Johnson, U.S.A.	28
J. H. Lacey, Great Britain	28
C. F. Gray, New Zealand	27½
Charles H. MacDonald, U.S.A.	27
George E. Preddy, U.S.A.	26
E. S. Lock, Great Britain	26
Joseph J. Foss, U.S.A.	26
Robert M. Hanson, U.S.A.	25

Musée de la Guerre Photo

Q. Identify the only two Luftwaffe pilots to attack Allied troops during the initial Normandy landings.

A. Colonel Josef "Pips" Priller and Sergeant Heinz Wodarczyk. All other German aircraft had been moved back from the French coast to avoid destruction from regular Allied bombing. The unit this lone Luftwaffe pair belonged to was the 26th Fighter Wing. Here Priller tells another Luftwaffe officer about the daring flight.

Bibliography

Ambrose, Stephen E. *The Supreme Commander: The War Years of General Dwight D. Eisenhower.* New York: Doubleday, 1970.

Angelucci, Enzo. *Airplanes from the Dawn of Flight to the Present Day.* New York: McGraw-Hill, 1973.

Aron, Robert. *De Gaulle Before Paris: The Liberation of France, June–August 1944.* New York: Putnam, 1962.

Aster, Sidney. *1939: The Making of the Second World War.* New York: Simon and Schuster, 1974.

Bazna, Elyesa. *I Was Cicero.* New York: Harper & Row, 1962.

Bekker, Cajus. *The Luftwaffe War Diaries.* New York: Doubleday, 1968.

————. *Hitler's Naval War.* New York: Doubleday, 1974.

Blair, Clay, Jr. *Silent Victory.* New York: Lippincott, 1975.

Boyington, Gregory. *Baa Baa Black Sheep.* New York: Putnam, 1958.

Bradley, Omar N. *A Soldier's Story.* New York: Henry Holt, 1951.

Brown, Anthony Cave. *Bodyguard of Lies.* New York: Harper & Row, 1975.

Buchanan, A. Russell. *The United States and World War II.* New York: Harper & Row, 1964.

Bullock, Alan. *Hitler—A Study in Tyranny.* New York: Harper & Row, 1963.

Butcher, Harry. *My Three Years with Eisenhower.* New York: Simon and Schuster, 1946.

Calvocoressi, Peter, and Wint, Guy. *Total War.* New York: Pantheon, 1972.

Catton, Bruce. *The War Lords of Washington.* New York: Harcourt Brace, 1948.

Churchill, Winston S. *The Second World War.* Boston: Houghton Mifflin, 1948–53.

Clark, Alan. *Barbarossa: The Russian-German Conflict, 1941–1945.* New York: Morrow, 1965.

Collier, Basil, *Japan at War.* London: Sidgwick and Jackson, 1975.

Collins, Larry, and Lapierre, Dominique. *Is Paris Burning?* New York: Simon and Schuster, 1965.

Daley, Robert. *An American Saga: Juan Trippe and His Pan American Empire.* New York: Random House, 1980.

Dean, John R. *The Strange Alliance: The Story of Our Efforts at Wartime Cooperation with Russia.* New York: Viking, 1947.

De Gaulle, Charles. *War Memoirs.* New York: Simon and Schuster, 1964.

Deighton, Len. *Blitzkrieg.* New York: Knopf, 1980.

Delmer, Sefton. *The Counterfeit Spy.* New York: Harper & Row, 1971.

Dissette, Edward, and Adamson, Hans Christian. *Guerrilla Submarines.* New York: Bantam Books, 1980.

Dulles, Allen W. *The Craft of Intelligence.* New York: Harper & Row, 1963.

————. *The Secret Surrender.* New York: Harper & Row, 1966.

Eisenhower, Dwight D. *Crusade in Europe.* New York: Avon, 1968.

Elson, Robert. *Prelude to War.* New York: Time/Life, 1976.

Epstein, Helen. *Children of the Holocaust.* New York: Putnam, 1979.

Essame, Hubert, and Belfield, E. M. G. *Normandy Bridgehead.* New York: Ballantine, 1970.

Farago, Ladislas. *The Broken Seal.* New York: Random House, 1967.

————. *The Game of the Foxes.* New York: McKay, 1971.

Fleming, Peter. *Operation Sea Lion.* New York: Simon and Schuster, 1957.

Ford, Corey. *Donovan of OSS.* Boston: Little, Brown, 1970.

Fuller, J. F. C. *The Second World War, 1939–1945.* New York: Duell, Sloan & Pearce, 1949.

Gavin, James M. *On to Berlin.* New York: Viking, 1978.

Goebbels, Joseph. *Diaries of Joseph Goebbels, 1942–1943.* New York: Doubleday, 1948.

Goralski, Robert. *World War II Almanac, 1939–1945.* New York: Putnam, 1981.

Hughes, Terry, and Costello, John. *The Battle of the Atlantic.* New York: Dial, 1977.

Innis, W. Joe, with Bunton, Bill. *In Pursuit of the Awa Maru.* New York: Bantam Books, 1981.

Irving, David. *The German Atomic Bomb.* New York: Simon and Schuster, 1968.

Jackson, Stanley. *The Savoy: The Romance of a Great Hotel.* London: Frederick Muller, 1964.

Jackson, W. G. F. *The Battle for Italy.* London: Batsford, 1967.

Kahn, David, *The Codebreakers.* New York: Macmillan, 1967.

Kaufman, Louis; Fitzgerald, Barbara; and Sewell, Tom. *Mo Berg: Athlete, Scholar, Spy.* Boston: Little, Brown, 1974.

Keil, Sally Van Wagenen. *Those Wonderful Women in Their Flying Machines.* New York: Rawson, Wade, 1979.

Kimmel, Husband E. *Admiral Kimmel's Story.* Chicago: Henry Regnery, 1955.

King, Ernest J., and Whitehill, W. M. *Fleet Admiral King.* New York: Norton, 1952.

Kitchen, Ruben P., Jr. *Pacific Carrier.* New York: Zebra Books, 1980.

Kowalski, Isaac. *A Secret Press in Nazi Europe.* New York: Shengold, 1978.

Kramarz, Joachim. *Stauffenberg: The Life and Death of an Officer.* London: Deutsch, 1967.

Lawson, Ted W. *Thirty Seconds over Tokyo.* New York: Random House, 1943.

Leahy, W. *I Was There.* New York: Whittlesey, 1950.

Le Vien, Jack, and Lord, John. *Winston Churchill: The Valiant Years.* New York: Bernard Geis, 1962.

Longmate, Norman. *If Britain Had Failed.* New York: Stein & Day, 1974.

Lord, Walter. *Day of Infamy.* New York: Henry Holt, 1957.

McKee, Alexander. *Last Round Against Rommel.* New York: New American Library, 1964.

Manchester, William. *American Caesar: Douglas MacArthur, 1880–1964.* Boston: Little, Brown, 1978.

Manvell, Roger, and Fraenkel, Heinrich. *The Canaris Conspiracy.* New York: McKay, 1969.

Marshall, Samuel. *Night Drop.* Boston: Little, Brown, 1962.

Mason, David. *Who's Who in World War II.* Boston: Little, Brown, 1978.

————. *U-Boat: The Secret Menace.* New York: Ballantine, 1968.

Michel, Henri. *The Shadow War.* New York: Harper & Row, 1973.

Michel, Jean. *Dora: The Nazi Concentration Camp Where Modern Space Technology Was Born and 30,000 Prisoners Died.* New York: Holt, Rinehart and Winston, 1980.

Mikesh, Robert C. *Japan's World War II Balloon Bomb Attacks on North America.* Washington: Smithsonian Institution Press, 1973.

Mollo, Andrew. *A Pictorial History of the SS.* New York: Bonanza, 1979.

Montagu, Ewen. *The Man Who Never Was.* Philadelphia: Lippincott, 1954.

Morella, Joe; Epstein, Edward Z.; and Griggs, John. *The Films of World War II.* New York: Citadel/Lyle Stuart, 1975.

Morison, Samuel E. *The History of United States Naval Operations in World War II.* 14 vols. Boston: Little, Brown, 1947–62.

Page, Geoffrey. *Tale of a Guinea Pig.* New York: Bantam, 1981.

Patton, George S., Jr. *War As I Knew It.* Boston: Houghton Mifflin, 1947.

Payne, Robert. *The Life and Death of Adolf Hitler.* New York: Praeger, 1973.

Pearcy, Arthur. *DC-3.* New York: Ballantine, 1975.

Peniakoff, Vladimir. *Popski's Private Army.* New York: Bantam, 1980.

Popov, Dusko. *Spy-Counterspy.* New York: Grosset & Dunlap, 1974.

Ryan, Cornelius. *The Longest Day.* New York: Simon and Schuster, 1959.

————. *A Bridge Too Far.* New York: Simon and Schuster, 1974.

————. *The Last Battle.* New York: Simon and Schuster, 1966.

Schaeffer, Heinz. *U-Boat 977.* New York: Norton, 1953.

Sherrod, Robert. *Tarawa.* New York: Duell, Sloan & Pearce, 1944.

Shirer, William L. *The Rise and Fall of the Third Reich.* New York: Simon and Schuster, 1960.

Simms, Edward H. *American Aces.* New York: Harper Brothers, 1958.

Smith, Liz. *The Mother Book.* New York: Doubleday, 1978.

Speer, Albert. *Inside the Third Reich.* New York: Avon, 1970.

Stagg, J. M. *Forecast for Overload.* New York: Norton, 1972.

Strong, Sir Kenneth. *Intelligence at the Top.* New York: Doubleday, 1969.

Sulzberger, C. L. *The American Heritage Picture History of World War II.* New York: American Heritage, 1966.

Sunderman, James F. *World War II in the Air.* New York: Franklin Watts, 1962.

Sutton, Horace. *Travelers.* New York: Morrow, 1980.

TerHorst, Jerald F., and Albertazzie, Ralph. *The Flying White House.* New York: Coward, McCann & Geoghegan, 1979.

Thomson, David. *Europe Since Napoleon.* New York: Knopf, 1960.

Toland, John. *The Last 100 Days.* New York: Random House, 1965.

Tregaskis, Richard. *Guadalcanal Diary.* New York: Random House, 1943.

Truman, Harry S. *Memoirs.* New York: Doubleday, 1958.

Wallechinsky, David; Wallace, Amy; and Wallace, Irving. *The People's Almanac Presents the Book of Predictions.* New York: Morrow, 1981.

Whiting, Charles. *Hitler's Werewolves.* New York: Bantam, 1973.

————. *The Hunt for Martin Bormann.* New York: Ballantine, 1973.

————. *Patton.* New York: Ballantine, 1971.

Wiener, Jan G. *The Assassination of Heydrich.* New York: Pyramid, 1969.

Williams, Eric. *The Wooden Horse.* New York: Bantam, 1980.

Winterbotham, Frederick W. *The Ultra Secret.* New York: Harper & Row, 1974.

Young, Desmond. *Rommel, the Desert Fox.* New York: Harper Brothers, 1950.

Index

Page numbers in *italics* denote illustrations